An Itinerary for New Testament Study

An Itinerary for
New Testament Study

Dieter Lührmann

SCM PRESS
London

TRINITY PRESS INTERNATIONAL
Philadelphia

Translated by John Bowden from the German
Auslegung des Neuen Testaments
published 1984 by Theologischer Verlag Zürich.

© Theologischer Verlag Zürich 1984

Translation © John Bowden 1989

First published 1989

SCM Press   Trinity Press International
26–30 Tottenham Road   3725 Chestnut Street
London N1 4BZ   Philadelphia, Pa. 19104

British Library Cataloguing in Publication Data

Lührmann, Dieter
    An itinerary for New Testament Study.
    1. Bible. N. T. Critics
    I. Title   II. Auslegung des neuen Testaments.
    English
    225.6

    ISBN 0–334–02076–X

Library of Congress Cataloging-in-Publication Data

Lührmann, Dieter.
    An itinerary for New Testament Study.

    Translation of: Auslegung des Neuen Testaments.
    1. Bible. N. T.—Criticism, interpretation etc.
I. Title
BS2364.2.L8413   1989   225.6′1   89–5024
ISBN 0–334–02076–X

Photoset by Input Typesetting Ltd
and printed in Great Britain by
The Camelot Press Ltd, Southampton

For Helmut Krämer

Contents

Preface to the English Edition

by J. L. Houlden, *Professor of Theology at King's College, London*

The scholarship of different countries has different excellences. Translation can make unfamiliar achievements and amenities more widely available, and may even encourage imitation and so convergence. English-speaking students of the New Testament have available to them a rich choice of recent works introducing them to the currently available skills used in the field. They also have collections of documents roughly contemporary with the New Testament and accounts of Christian origins.

Nevertheless, for certain purposes the 'right' introductory textbook has been lacking. To fill the gap, it is good to offer a German-style handbook. Its positive value twofold. It is a clearly ordered handbook to New Testament studies and the student who masters it will have set off on a profitable journey. And in its conception of literary source criticism, history of religions and theology as the New Testament student's business, it illustrates the strengths (as well as the limitations) of such work in its German form, with the immensely impressive German tradition of scholarship at its back.

January 1989   Leslie Houlden

1   The New Testament

1.1   The canon

1.1.1   The basic problem

Christianity, especially in its Protestant form, is committed to history from the very beginning. But there is not a new book at its beginning, as was later the case with Islam, whose founder Muhammad set down his new religion in the Qur'an, following the model of both Judaism and Christianity (even if a critical examination distinguishes some later tradition from the original text).

Rather, early Christianity first managed with the book which was later called the 'Old Testament'. In it Christians found all that they were looking for: the will of God, the history of the world from the beginning and therefore also its goal, in the time of those on whom the ends of the times had come (I Cor.10.11). The form and extent of the text which they used was that of the Greek version, the 'Septuagint'. And this 'Old' Testament has also been read until modern times as a Christian book, before as a result of historical criticism it seemed to be more a holy book of the Jewish religion than of the Christian religion (see 1.1.5).

1.1.2   The collecting of the Christian writings

Early Christianity began only gradually to collect its own writings. Towards the end of the first century there was a collection of the writings left by Paul, letters from the phase of his activity around the Aegean, and thus from within a limited geographical area: ten letters to seven communities and to Philemon; it still lacked the 'Pastoral Letters' to Timothy and Titus and the Letter to the Hebrews, which was later incorporated into the New Testament because it was thought to have been written by Paul.

The Gospels also came into being in the last third of the first century;

about a generation after the events it was necessary to preserve what was known in written form. From the beginning it was felt to be a problem that four Gospels had been incorporated into the New Testament. That shows how open the Jesus tradition still was at this time, and even in the second century one comes across a still surviving oral tradition and other Gospels which were not included in the later New Testament. The author of the Third Gospel finally continued his work by describing the beginnings of the church in his 'Acts of the Apostles' as the way in which the gospel spread from its beginnings in Jerusalem to Paul's arrival in Rome. This corresponds with the programme outlined in Acts 1.8: 'You will be my witnesses in Jerusalem and throughout Judaea and Samaria and to the ends of the world.' The rest of the writings of the New Testament, the so-called 'Catholic letters' and the Revelation of John, over whose inclusion in the collection there was the longest dispute, did not come into being earlier, but mostly later. The writings collected in the 'New Testament' all date from the period between about 50 and about 135 CE – a short span of time, compared with the interval of several centuries between the earliest and latest parts of the Old Testament.

We know little about how these writings were actually used until well into the second century, and that is also true of the ordering of worship in this period. Although the writings themselves suggest some links with worship, we are really completely in the dark here. One reason for this may be that this early Christianity spread so quickly in all directions that it did not have a single shape or form from the beginning, but only attempted to achieve this unity later. This is a problem which still occurs today in the manifold traditions of worldwide Christianity.

1.1.3   The question of the basic writings

A need to establish authoritative scriptures first arose in the second half of the second century as a result of the activity of Marcion. He questioned whether one could in fact learn anything about the real God from the writings of the Old Testament; this God had first been proclaimed by Jesus. Marcion now wanted to base the church only on Jesus and Paul, with a revised version of the Gospel of Luke and the letters of Paul, gospel and apostle, as the two parts of this New Testament.

H. von Campenhausen, *The Origin of the Christian Bible*, A.& C.Black and Fortress Press 1972;

B.Metzger, *The Canon of the New Testament*, Oxford University Press 1987;

P.R.Ackroyd and C.F.Evans (eds.), *The Cambridge History of the Bible* I, Cambridge University Press 1970, ch.10 (R.M.Grant);

W.R.Farmer and D.M.Farkasfalvy, *The Formation of the New Testament Canon*, Paulist Press 1983.

'What this inevitably meant for the second-century church it is now hardly possible to appreciate. She had lost her "scriptures"; at one and the same moment her proud claim to be the religion of the most ancient wisdom and the religion of historical fulfilment were both rendered invalid' (Campenhausen, 151). The excommunication of Marcion might have removed the danger for the moment, but in the long run it could not answer the question which he had put to the church about its foundations.

The first comprehensive outline of a clarification comes from Irenaeus of Lyons. According to him the essential content of the 'canon of truth' or 'of faith' (Latin *regula veritatis* or *fidei*), the tradition of the church which goes back via the apostles to Christ, is: 1. that God is creator of this world; 2. that Jesus is the Son of this God, was capable of suffering, and did in fact suffer.

So Irenaeus really did not need a 'New Testament' as a book, but was asking about the scriptures in which this original tradition is contained. The reason for this is that others were basing their teaching on scriptures for which they also claimed originality. For Irenaeus the Old Testament belongs among the scriptures which verify the *regula fidei* (against Marcion); like the tradition before him he interprets the Old Testament as having the New Testament as its goal: in other words, in fact in the light of the New Testament.

But where do we find the real evidence for this fulfilment? According to Irenaeus this is: 1. the teaching of all the apostles according to the four Gospels and the Acts of the Apostles; 2. the discourses of the Lord; 3. the apostolic letters of Paul (now including the Pastoral Letters).

It is surprising that the Gospels and Acts are put first, as the Gospels are not seen primarily as an account of the teaching of Jesus but of the teaching of the apostles. Irenaeus holds firm to the four Gospels, though they cause him a problem, whereas on the one hand Marcion only used the Gospel of Luke and on the other hand in the second century there were attempts to present the one gospel by working the four Gospels together into a single book. (The best known attempt of this kind is Tatian's *Diatessaron*, which was canonical in the Syrian church up to the fifth century as *the* gospel.)

The second group, 'discourses of the Lord', looks like a relic; this material is no longer understood as oral tradition but as the discourses of Jesus contained in the Gospels, above all the Sermon on the Mount in Matt. 5-7. Since there is dispute as to what Jesus said, as a counter to the free tradition of the words of Jesus which is still continuing their content must be fixed in writing. But this makes all the collections of sayings of Jesus outside the Gospels inauthentic.

The third group, the apostolic letters of Paul, had already existed for some time as a collection of letters; its value, among other things, lay in the fact that in his letters Paul had already dealt with all kinds of heresies – and now provided a model for dealing with such controversies in the present.

So this collection of 'canonical' writings enables Irenaeus to identify the sources of the *regula fidei* as the teaching of the church going back to the apostles: the one truth 'which the prophets foretold and Christ carried out and the apostles handed down and the church proclaims to its children throughout the world' (*Epideixis* 98). In addition to the writings mentioned above (Gospels, Acts, letters of Paul), Irenaeus also cites I Peter and the first two letters of John, but does not give them canonical status (which he also denies to the Revelation of John).

In the subsequent period we can notice an increase in the extent of these writings: a Gospel of Peter is occasionally added to the Gospels, a III Corinthians and a Letter to the Laodiceans to the letters of Paul; the Letter to the Hebrews is thought to have been composed by Paul. There are also II Peter, the Letter of Barnabas, the Letter of Jude, I Clement, a Kerygma Petrou; and among the revelations, in addition to the Revelation of John, there is an Apocalypse of Peter and the Shepherd of Hermas. However, anything beyond the nucleus mentioned by Irenaeus (four Gospels, Acts, thirteen letters of Paul) largely continued to be disputed.

The 'Muratorian Canon', which was produced around 200, probably in Rome as a more or less official listing for the Roman community of this time, mentions, in addition to the four Gospels, Acts and the thirteen letters of Paul: the Letter of Jude, two letters of John, the Wisdom of Solomon and the Revelations of John and Peter, but it disputes the place of a Letter to the Laodiceans and a Letter to the Alexandrians, and of the Shepherd of Hermas (there is an English translation of the text of the canon in E.Hennecke, W.Schneemelcher, R.McL. Wilson, *New Testament Apocrypha* I, Lutterworth Press and Westminster Press 1963, 42ff.).

The concern that can already be recognized here to close the canon and exclude writings which others included in it continues in the third century. The principles which become established are age and reliability, i.e. to some degree a 'historical' principle, and the acceptance of the writings in all the churches of the time. There is most dispute over the Revelation of John.

In the fourth century, when Christianity became an imperial church, the canon of the New Testament was fixed in the form with which we are familiar: four Gospels (there were a great many explanations of why there was this number of them), Acts, the seven so-called 'Catholic Letters' (orientated on the 'pillars' of Gal.2.9: James, Peter, John and Jude, who according to the prescript is in fact the brother of James). In most manuscripts the thirteen letters of Paul and the Letter to the Hebrews come after them, and finally the Revelation of John as the only apocalypse. However, the memory remained alive that even in the fourth century the place of some writings in the collection was not undisputed: Hebrews, James, II Peter, II and III John, Jude and the Revelation of John.

Together with the Old Testament, the New Testament marked out in this way formed the one Bible. From Irenaeus onwards its focal point lay in the teaching of the church, but this in turn had to be shown to be in accordance with the Bible. Attempts at reform within the church took their start from the contradiction between the teaching and practice of the church on the one hand and what was read in this Bible as original tradition on the other. So with the canon the church had at the same time created its own criticism.

1.1.4   Reformation criticism of the canon

There was no dispute in the Middle Ages over the extent of the canon, although one could read in the Latin translation of the *Church History* of the church father Eusebius of Caesarea (died 339) and in Jerome (died 420) that the canonicity of the seven works mentioned above had been doubted. When Erasmus of Rotterdam (see 2.1.3) published his New Testament in Greek (1516), he added introductions to the individual New Testament writings in which he highlighted such information. However, he did not draw the conclusion that the canon should be reduced, but included all twenty-seven works, and this extent became permanently established, so that though they differ over the Old Testament, Protestant, Anglican, Roman Catholic and Orthodox churches all refer to the same New Testament.

Initially, however, this question of the extent of the New Testament was quite open. Luther, who translated Erasmus's Greek text and also made use of Erasmus's introductions in his prefaces to the individual writings, gave a special place to the four works Hebrews, James, Jude and the Revelation of John, which they still hold today in Luther Bibles.

He transposed Hebrews and James, contrary to the traditional order, to the end of the New Testament, before Jude and the Revelation of John, and numbered only the first twenty-three writings consecutively in the table of contents, adding these four without numbers. In so doing he distinguished between the 'main books' of the New Testament and these four, because there was doubt as to whether they had been written by the authors whose names they bore.

There was no such criticism of the other three writings which had been disputed in the early church (Luther thought that II Peter and II and III John had been written by Peter and John respectively). Historical doubt was welcome to Luther where he had reservations about the content for theological reasons; there was no such doubt where he had no reservations as to content.

Unfortunately Luther's prefaces are no longer included in editions of the Luther Bible: an English translation can be found in H.T.Lehmann and E.T.Bachmann, *Luther's Works*, Vol.35, Fortress Press 1960.

Whereas Luther only partially accepted the criticism of the seven works disputed in the early church, where it matched his theological interests, this criticism had a very wide influence among the humanists, and also within continuing Roman Catholic theology. So in 1546 the Council of Trent did not just have Luther in view when it listed individually the writings which belonged in the Bible, in contrast to the councils of the early church, none of which had been concerned with the canon. The title apostle is expressly repeated in the case of each of the authors of the disputed works; the Latin text, not the Greek form, is made binding.

There were objections to this definition of the extent of the canon from the Lutheran side not only in the case of the Old Testament but also in the case of the New. The church's right to add the seven disputed works to the Old Testament canon was challenged, and they were called 'apocryphal' or 'deutero-canonical' works. Whereas in the case of the Old Testament the books contained in the Septuagint that were not in the Hebrew Bible were actually called 'Apocrypha', the distinction being made on the basis of language, this was not possible with the New Testament, since all the writings, including those which were disputed, had been handed down in Greek. Here the decisive question was whether the writings in question also undoubtedly came from their alleged authors – in other words, this was a 'historical' principle.

Despite the degree to which 'scripture' is regarded as the sole criterion for the teaching of the church in the Lutheran tradition, the Lutheran confessional writings do not say anything about the extent or textual form of this 'scripture', and that distinguishes them not only from the Catholic tradition, which is related to the Council of Trent, but also from the Reformed tradition, since its confessional writings often contain lists of canonical books. 'Scripture' for the Lutheran tradition is something like the Luther Bible, or the editions of the Hebrew Old and the Greek New Testaments, but this is not more closely defined in any way (though later Lutheran dogmatic theologians make the attempt). The concept of scripture is not based on a formal canonical principle but on a qualitative definition of what the Bible contains. Perhaps this openness saved the canon in the face of the historical criticism of the subsequent period, which was not only directed against the seven works disputed in the early church but also cast doubts on the alleged authorship of further works. For Luther, Judas, Annas, Pilate or Herod could be authors; if they preached Christ one could confidently use their books. So he was not concerned with any special authority of the author but with the content: 'what preaches or furthers Christ', according to the preface to the Letter of James which is critical about the letter; or 'law and gospel'. These two entities are distributed over the Old and New Testaments, but not in such a way that the Old Testament contains the law and the New the gospel: both are contained in both, even if there is more law in the Old Testament and more gospel in the New. So to find 'law and gospel' in the Bible is the task of exegesis; in Luther, too, the norm of the canon is church teaching, which has to authenticate itself by the Bible. The new development is that this norm is now defined in a different way; critical exegesis remains an open task, that of seeking whether such a definition does justice to the Bible.

1.1.5 The canon as a problem of historical criticism

In the subsequent period the humanists' criticism of the extent of the Bible continued to be remembered; in addition, the insight was strengthened that the Bible is a book which came into being through history, and was written by different authors at different times. Johann Salomo Semler (1725-1791) was the first to mention this problem in his 'Treatise on the Free Investigation of the Canon' (1771-6).

Semler distinguishes between Word of God and Holy Scripture. Here conceptually he is in the Lutheran tradition, but he regards the Word of God as that which can also serve for 'moral improvement' in the present, and on that basis he criticizes the Revelation of John in particular. In his view the canon goes back to a consensus of the churches, and therefore is not an authority foreordained before church history; so every Christian has the right to investigate and assess any writing freely, but within the private sphere; for public worship the official teaching of the church continues to remain in force. This division

between private and public was to have serious consequences for
Protestant tradition, as there was less and less official church teaching
in the later period; at the same time the question of what is valid in the
Bible was raised under the criterion of moral truth. Thus the Bible has
authority only to the degree to which it accords with reason.

A little later a programmatic distinction was made in the inaugural
lecture by John Philipp Gabler (1753-1826) at the University of Altdorf
in 1787, between the theology of the Old Testament and the theology
of the New Testament, and in this way the unity of the Bible was put in
question.

For an introduction to these two figures and extracts from their works see
W.G.Kümmel, *The New Testament. The History of the Investigation of its
Problems*, Abingdon Press and SCM Press 1973: for Semler, 62-9; for Gabler,
98-101.

In the nineteenth century, 'Old Testament' and 'New Testament' then
increasingly became established as two independent disciplines, and
whether the Old Testament belonged in the Bible became a fundamental
question. Paragraph 115 of Friedrich Schleiermacher's (1768-1834)
reforming work *A Brief Account of Theological Study... to serve
as Introductory Lectures* reads: 'It will probably soon be generally
recognized that the Jewish codex (= the Old Testament) does not
contain a normal account of specifically Christian principles of faith.
But that does not mean that to depart from the use of the early church,
which combines the Old Testament with the New into a totality, the
Bible, is necessary – though it must also remain permissible.'

For the text see F.D.E.Schleiermacher, *A Brief Outline on the Study of
Theology*, John Knox Press 1966.

For the New Testament the problem became more acute when nineteenth-century criticism raised doubts as to whether other works than
those disputed in the early church (see 2.4.1) had actually been written
by the authors mentioned in the text (e.g. Paul in the Pastoral Letters)
and now went on to talk of deutero-Paulines. The criterion of historical
authenticity thus put the authority and truth of these writings in
question.

At the same time it emerged that the writings brought together in the
canon of the New Testament cannot all be described as the earliest
Christian writings that have been preserved, and that both among the
'Apostolic Fathers' and among the 'Apocrypha' there are texts which
can be dated before late texts of the New Testament.

The term 'Apostolic Fathers' is used to denote a group of writings
(their extent has not been fixed precisely) which include letters of

Bishop Ignatius of Antioch (written about 110), I Clement (a letter from the Roman community to Corinth, written about 96), the Didache (a collection of pieces of church teaching which was probably written during the first century) and further texts predominantly from the first half of the second century, to which the Pastorals or II Peter are also dated.

The most convenient edition of the Apostolic Fathers in English is *Early Christian Writings. The Apostolic Fathers*, Penguin Books [2]1987. For parallel Greek and English texts see the edition of the Apostolic Fathers in the Loeb Classical Library (two vols.), Heinemann 1912.
For a commentary on the letters of Ignatius of Antioch see William R.Schoedel, *Ignatius of Antioch*, Hermeneia, Fortress Press 1985.

Whereas in the case of the Old Testament the term Apocrypha denotes a clearly defined group of writings (those in the Septuagint over and above the Hebrew Bible), in the case of the New Testament its scope is much wider, and in fact it denotes all texts in the form of gospels, acts or letters of apostles, or apocalypses which are regarded as traditions from the early period of Christianity.

The classic edition of these writings is M.R.James, *The Apocryphal New Testament*, Oxford University Press 1924. But see especially E.Hennecke, W.Schneemelcher and R.McL.Wilson, *New Testament Apocrypha* (two volumes), Lutterworth Press and Westminster Press 1963, 1965.

Here, too, some texts like the Gospel of Thomas or the Gospel of Peter probably go back to the first half of the second century, but probably not into the first.

Whereas books entitled *Introduction to the New Testament* usually discuss only the books in the canon and the origin of the canon, P.Vielhauer has also included the Apostolic Fathers and the Apocrypha in his *History of Early Christian Literature* (1975).

The historical problem of the canon is the question how particular writings were singled out as the New Testament; the theological problem is the question how these writings form a unity and how New and Old Testaments belong together as the one canon (see 3.4.4).

C.F.Evans, *Is Holy Scripture Christian?*, SCM Press 1971;
John Barton, *Oracles of God*, Darton, Longman and Todd 1986;
id., *People of the Book?*, SPCK 1988.

1.2   The text

1.2.1   The two basic types

In the New Testament a distinction should be made between two basic types of texts. The first type consists of texts in which a narrator reports in the past tense something that has taken place (Gospels, Acts); only rarely (e.g. Luke 1.1-4; John 20.30f.) is there an explicit account of the approach and purpose of the text. This type is predominant in the Old Testament, where not only the five books of the Pentateuch and the historical books but also the prophetic books depict the past for a particular present.

A new development from the Old Testament which occurs in the New Testament is the appearance of texts of a second type, letters in which an author explicitly addresses a particular contemporary audience in order to take up particular problems and discuss these problems with them – the problems may arise from a specific situation or be general ones. Strictly speaking, this is the case only with the authentic letters of Paul, where we know the author and those whom he was originally addressing, but it served as a model for other letters which were written later. However, the more independent these are of a particular situation, the closer they usually are to another part of the Old Testament, the wisdom literature.

The Apocalypse of John should also be included in this second type, since according to its framework (1.3; 22.18f.) it is a book addressed by an author to readers and begins with letters, even if it then predominantly consists of a prophetic account of future events.

This distinction is merely meant to indicate basic types. Paul, too, reports past events in a letter (Gal.1.13-2.31), and in so doing provides an important source for the history of earliest Christianity; on the other hand the Gospels and Acts contain elements which are to be classified as the second type – Acts even contains letters (e.g. Acts 15.23-29).

1.2.2   Narrative texts

This distinction between two basic types leads to various questions of principle about the exegesis of particular texts. In the first type we have to note a triangular relationship between author, reader and what is reported; here, however, the reader is very much in the background. Within the text itself the reader is addressed only in the surprising interjection in Mark 13.14. But like us, the original readers will already have felt that Jesus or the apostles were speaking to them wherever in a narrative Jesus or the apostles address their audience as 'you'.

The Gospels and Acts presuppose that the readers already have some knowledge about what they are being told (this is explicitly the case in Luke 1.4), so they are not providing basic information. What the authors want to communicate to their readers is on the one hand a confirmation of their knowledge and on the other hand additions to it and extensions of it (at times even corrections to it).

We can see the relationship between author and reader wherever the author thinks that he must give his readers information without which they will not be able to understand what he tells them (e.g. Mark 7.3f. or 2.18a on Jewish customs; John 5.2 on local features in Jerusalem). Something of this kind only becomes necessary when the story is no longer narrating immediately past happenings, but has been retold many times, so that the possibility of a lack of knowledge among the new audience in some areas must now be taken into account.

This is already exegesis of an existing text in a very simple form. Present-day exegesis, too, first of all consists in giving readers and hearers information that is no longer directly accessible about persons, groups, places, customs, etc., and also about special meanings of words. Even the simple retelling of a text cannot be done without such incidental remarks, however exact or inexact they may be.

In this first type of text it is necessary to ask about:
– The place and time of the action, whether they are indicated in the text or not;
– The characters who appear, whether they appear as a group, as typical persons, or as individual figures;
– the functions of the people who appear in the story and possibly the way in which they are characterized by the narrator;
– the course of actions which is depicted, whether this follows a straight line or there are elements in it which hold the action back;
– additional information or specific comments which the author introduces;
– the purpose of the action as the author envisages it and the preparation for this purpose in the story itself;
– the connection between the story and the broader course of action in the book as a whole, and the position of the individual story in the book.

An *a priori* distinction has to be made between the text and the events narrated in the text. The two are not simply identical; this can easily be made clear if one tells the same story from the perspective of other people mentioned in it, provided that one can keep to the course of the story and also to the statements which appear 'literally' in it (e.g. a dispute from the perspective of the Pharisees or one of the stories in Acts 16-19 from the perspective of the Jewish synagogue in which Paul had appeared); in that case one has only to alter the tacit or explicit evaluations which it contains.

In this way we come up even more clearly against the fact that the New Testament authors are interested only in Jesus or the apostles. This makes their account 'one-sided' and does not allow any independent interest in the other figures, even the opponents. This phenomenon as such is not, of course, peculiar to the New Testament texts; we come across it every day, for example, even in what seem to be the most objective statements in news broadcasts.

But this interest is not just limited to reporting what happened 'then' in Galilee, Jerusalem or Ephesus. The aim of the authors is, rather, to narrate something which applies to the present. It coincides with the interest of the readers who, while wanting to learn about the past, also want to hear something which applies to the present. This phenomenon, too, applies to all kinds of history writing; since the rise of the historical consciousness in modern times it is possible to take account of it.

So texts of this first type are always to be read on two levels, first as to the relationship between author and readers, and then as to the relationship between the author (and also the readers) and the past event which is reported. However, for us (though this is already true from that point in time at which others than the readers originally envisaged by the author pick up his book) the relationship between author and reader is also in the past, so that there are three levels; in addition to the relationships I have mentioned there is the relationship between the text which a particular author once wrote for particular readers and ourselves, to whom this text has come via a long intermediate history.

In principle, the place of the exegete in the triangle of author, reader and what is reported is primarily that of the reader, as the one who encounters the texts, though in another period. Only through the text does he or she then go on to encounter the author. So exegesis of the text begins with the reader, but becomes a retelling in which information needed by readers of a particular time is added and in which again what is 'valid' is translated in terms of a particular present.

Here we have no as it were independent access to the events which these texts report. We have no contemporary sources from Jews or Romans, who would certainly not only have evaluated the events reported in a different way but would also have put them in another overall context. So we cannot attempt to reproduce the relationship between the author and the event he reports without the New Testament texts, no matter how often that happens by the provision of apparently objective accounts of events.

1.2.3 Argumentative texts

Among texts of the second type, the authentic letters of Paul should be mentioned in first place. Here we meet an author whose biography we know relatively well, and we can reconstruct the situation of those to whom the letters were originally addressed from the questions discussed in them and sometimes also with the help of Acts. One slight qualification should be made, namely that the letters of Paul have come down to us only as part of a collection made by someone else, so that we cannot rule out a later revision here and there. Nevertheless, the relationship between the author and the readers is very much clearer here in the texts themselves, as is already evident from the frequency with which 'I/we' and 'you' occurs in them.

For later readers, however, the problem arises, almost more than in the first type, that one has to acquire further information which is not directly contained in the text itself, because the author shares this with his readers and therefore does not really need to mention it. For example, the Corinthians know what they wrote to Paul about marriage, divorce and remaining unmarried (I Cor.7.1), or the Galatians know the content of that 'other gospel' (Gal.1.6-9) which so led them astray.

But this knowledge is a presupposition for understanding the text, since it relates to what Paul is replying. That in fact there is a wide range of plausible reconstructions of the situation in exegetical literature does not tell against this, but is just an indication of how much the texts themselves can come alive simply from the author-reader relationship.

A second group in this basic type of text comprises letters which claim fictitiously to have an author-reader relationship in the past, but in reality have been written by an unknown author at a later time for a circle of readers who in this case are equally unknown. So these texts, for example the Pastoral Letters, have a similarly twofold level to texts of the first type. Here, however, we are not dealing with an event in the past but with the authority of Paul from the past, which is claimed in connection with problems in the present.

The author who conceals himself behind Paul will certainly not have thought that he was writing anything other than what Paul would have written had he still been alive. At the same time we must suppose that the assumed situation of the past allows us to make inferences about the present situation of the author and reader; here too, more information is given in the text itself about the fictitious reader than Paul would have needed.

Finally, not very different from this second group is a third, which with or without any fictional element in fact dispenses with any author-reader relationship, and which as in Ephesians or Hebrews, but also in James, presents theological themes which are apparently independent of any situation. Here too, of course, we can see that such texts came into being at a particular time in the face of particular problems. But that is very much less important for the interpretation of such texts than for example in the case of the authentic letters of Paul.

Only this third group of the second type can be compared with the writings in the wisdom literature of the Old Testament, with which the texts in question also have a large number of points of contact in both form and content. This is by no means fortuitous.

In the interpretation of texts of this second type we need to ask about:
- the thesis put forward by the author;
- the arguments with which he arrives at his thesis and defends it;
- the problem to which his argument relates, whether this is specific, or a universal and fundamental problem;
- the wider horizon against which the author sets the problem;
- the tone of his arguments, whether he is approving or polemical:
- his manner of arguing, whether he builds up an argument sentence by sentence, uses comparisons or puts rhetorical questions to the readers;
- the basis of the argument, whether this is the experience of the readers, or recollection, or authoritative quotations, or an indication of consequences;
- the connection of the individual text with the wider context of the letter in which it is located, whether a problem regularly returns or whether the basis and mode of the argument remain the same.

The thesis and the course and mode of the argument allow us to draw conclusions about the opposing position, whether this is actual or theoretical. However, we may not simply formulate this position as the author does; occasionally we may identify antitheses which are deliberately very polemical or caricatures. The readers of the time were less interested in the opposing position, which they knew, than in the view of the author, who used an exaggeration of his opponent's position to challenge them to adopt his own. To this degree any reader is again put in the situation of those to whom the work was originally addressed in assessing thesis and argumentation.

The question of what is 'valid' is initially easier to answer here than in the first basic type, that of narrative texts, as the author in question is himself concerned to formulate what is valid. However, as in the first basic type, it is again the case that what is valid first presents itself to us in historical terms as what was valid then (or what was thought to have been valid then), and this has to be related in turn to our present situation.

Here again these texts cannot be retold without incidental comments which make problems of a past time easier to understand by using analogies with problems in our own present experience and in which specific problems in a particular situation are interpreted as being universal and timeless. Like the Pharisees in the Gospels, so too in the retelling Paul's opponents can be possibilities in the present.

For all these questions English and American readers will find D.L.Aune, *The New Testament in its Literary Environment*, Westminster Press 1987 and James Clarke 1988, a useful study.

1.2.4 Translating the texts

All the writings of the New Testament were originally written in Greek, including the Gospels, though their origin lies in the Aramaic mother tongue of Jesus and his first disciples. Translations were already made in the Jesus tradition; only in very few places here does the use of Aramaic or Hebrew words come through, and then they are mostly provided with a translation. Above all in the Gospel of Mark the syntax is more reminiscent of Hebrew grammar than Greek (the verb put first; a sentence construction like Mark 2.23a). There is a model for this process of translation in the rendering of the Hebrew Old Testament into Greek, and the linguistic style of the Septuagint influenced the authors of the New Testament writings in both vocabulary and sentence structure; even if they were writing in Greek, they were influenced by the language of their sacred writings.

Any translation, even one's own, is an interpretation of the text that has been translated: understanding the text and rendering it in one's own language condition each other. The German tradition (especially the Protestant tradition) is shaped by the language of the Luther Bible, which in turn has influenced the German language, and the same is true of the King James Version in the English-speaking world. Revision of these texts in recent years has brought out some problems, particularly the change in the meaning of particular words since the time the original translations were made (e.g. 'pious' in the sense of 'upright, righteous, just', cf. translations of Luke 18.9) and the way in which the translation is shaped throughout by dogmatic considerations (e.g. 'the Son of Man' in terms of the doctrine of two natures as a complementary term to 'Son of God').

Both these points also indicate problems of contemporary translations as to which words or what levels of language enter into the translation and how far a quite particular understanding of the text and Bible as a whole is involved in the translation (cf. the rendering of *euangelion* as 'good news' or varying translations of I Thess.4.1 in which one can see quite different understandings of Paul's ethics). Even a 'literal' translation is not free of such problems, since it is specifically the words which say roughly the same thing in our language that are put in question: corresponding words in English or German certainly do not have the associations that the Greek words have, and the history of the Bible in English or German has itself given certain words particular associations (e.g. 'faith' in current language).

Over recent years a whole series of new translations has been produced, including revisions of the Luther Bible and the King James Version. For all their difference in matters of principle they have in common the fact that they are based on the Greek text of the latest edition of Nestle (see 2.1.5) and at least draw on the *Lexicon* edited by Walter Bauer.

W.Bauer, W.F.Arndt and F.W.Gingrich, *A Greek-English Lexicon of the New Testament and Other Early Christian Writings*, Chicago University Press ²1979.

Since Bauer does not simply give translations of words, but arranges the material by content, the problem of interpretation by translation arises again here (cf. 811, where Bauer leaves open the understanding of Rom.10.4, going against a broad consensus of exegetes); the vocabulary shows very close affinities to the linguistic tradition of dogmatics (cf. in particular the translation of 'good news').

Thus simply as the result of a comparison of various translations, the question of making one's own translation proves to be the question of what is 'really' there. A translation of one's own must correct itself during the process of understanding the text, as the translation in fact reflects a particular understanding; and one's own translation must be determined by its purpose or those to whom the translation is addressed. Retelling the text oneself is a good test, and at the same time the most difficult task.

Another aid to translation is a specialist grammar. The standard one is F.W.Funk's English version of F.Blass and E.Debrunner, *A Greek Grammar of the New Testament and Other Early Christian Writings*, Chicago University Press 1961. Those who read German should know that the fifteenth German edition of 1979 has been completely revised throughout by F.Rehkopf.

Here, too, of course it is evident that grammatical understanding and interpretation of the content influence each other. Measured by the grammar of classical Greek texts the Greek of the New Testament writings is certainly less precise; but that does not mean that it has no rules and is inaccurate.

Finally, there are concordances, i.e. listings of the occurrences of Greek words in the New Testament:

The standard concordance for the Greek New Testament is W.F.Moulton and A.S.Geden, *A Concordance to the Greek New Testament*, T.& T.Clark ³1926. There are also concordances available for the various English translations, from the King James Version to the Revised Standard Version and the Jerusalem Bible.

With the help of such a concordance it is possible to compare how the author in question uses the same word elsewhere, but also whether a word belongs in a particular word-field, so that one can always remember the wider context of this word-field along with the individual words. The associations of a Greek word can be quite different from those of a similar word in our language. Here, too, the relationships one establishes to other words and other texts are of course already a piece of interpretation. So all in all translation comes at the beginning of understanding the text, and at the same time it reflects newly-gained understanding; it is simultaneously both alien (in that it renders a text which originally someone other than the translator formulated in a foreign language) and familiar (in that it is an appropriation of this alien text).

1.3   Exegesis

1.3.1   The basic problem

While the basic question of what we call exegesis or interpretation can be put very simply: 'What is in the text?', 'What does the text tell me?', the question itself is not very simple. It is certainly aimed at making the text present and at a personal relationship to the text, regardless of whether or not the 'me' is stressed, but it has been posed in different ways at different times, and even now is asked in different ways.

One might represent the average interest, say, with the two questions 'What happened?' and 'What must I do?', i.e. as being historical and ethical, but even these questions are not clear in themselves, as they will be put from a series of different contexts. Personal interest is shaped by the traditions from which one comes, in which one has learned to read biblical texts, and by the discussion of these traditions and the role in which the texts appear, depending on whether they are felt to be threatening or liberating.

This is above all connected with the question of the status of the biblical texts, whether they are understood as a primary orientation for life; as a legitimation of one's own way of life or that of a group; as legitimation used by parents, communities and churches which is open to criticism; as part of the conditions of the world in which we live; or any other possibilities one might think of.

1.3.2   Exegesis as a scholarly discipline

Scholarly exegesis, too, cannot escape the question of what is valid at a particular time, even if it should want to, nor has it ever done so. It does not have a neutral standpoint of scientific or historical objectivity, but is involved in the process of understanding which I have mentioned, albeit at the level of reflection. The way in which people have looked for what was valid for their time and the way in which they have posed their questions has been different at different times.

Five main phases can be identified in the history of the Protestant interpretation of the Bible, all of which have had an effect on our present-day reading of the Bible, whether 'naive' or 'scholarly'. These tend to overlap:
– the Reformation, for which the newly discovered doctrine of justifi-cation under the key words 'law and gospel' was the key to the Bible as a whole and thus also the criterion for qualitative evaluations in the Bible;
– pietism, which sought the promise of the certainty of personal salvation in the biblical texts;
– the Enlightenment, for which the key and criterion was the correspon-dence between the biblical texts and general truths of reason on the one hand, and the quest for moral truths on the other;
– the historical theology of the nineteenth century (see 2.4), which investigated that which could be verified historically and could not be derived;
– theological exegesis in connection with dialectical theology (see 3.1), which asked about the alien Word of God which means grace, but above all judgment.

These – very roughly – are the various interests, and if what I observed at 1.3.1 is correct, above all the third and the fourth have established themselves.

Histories of interpretation
W.G.Kümmel, *The New Testament. The History of the Investigation of its Problems*, Abingdon Press and SCM Press 1973;

Robert M.Grant and David Tracy, *A Short History of the Interpretation of the Bible*, revised edition Fortress Press and SCM Press 1984;
R.Morgan with J.Barton, *Biblical Interpretation*, Oxford University Press 1988.

Since the development of modern scholarship, scholarly exegesis has been understood to be a form of interpretation the principles of which correspond to the general scientific principles of freedom and criticism. Both words refer to the same process: freedom is gained by the criticism of already existing authorities, in this context the doctrine of the church, and this creates truth which has a foundation and can be verified. Theology takes part in the development of the sciences and has its place in the disciplines of universities, but it always understands that it has to have practical realization in the church. The nineteenth century brought an irrevocable separation between the natural sciences and the humanities as two fundamentally different ways of understanding reality. For the natural sciences, reality can in principle be explained in its own terms; scientific results are evident if they can be tested by anyone at any time in an experiment. So the scientific method comprises attempts that can be repeated. By contrast, for the humanities present reality is to be understood from the history which determines the present; because its subject, history, is not itself present, the results of the humanities can only have a greater or lesser degree of probability, though this probability grows, the more individual phenomena fit into an overall picture. The method is characterized by the presuppositions that only what is possible now is historically conceivable, and that all events can be derived from causes within history itself.

Given this alternative, theology was of course on the side of the humanities and defines itself as historical theology, in a way formulated most evocatively by Ernst Troeltsch (see 2.4.2.2). How fundamental this alternative was can be studied in the dispute over Darwinism, which was concerned with the 'truth' of the Bible. Which was the correct explanation of the origin of life: science or the biblical creation narrative? How exegesis developed within the humanities as historical criticism is the theme of the second part of this book.

Since the humanities were understood as historical disciplines, philosophy became the history of philosophy, literary criticism became the history of literature, and so on. The confidence in the meaning of history which supported historicism of this kind can again be studied in Ernst Troeltsch, but it succumbed to a relativism which only saw a juxtaposition of facts without making values possible. The sense of the meaninglessness of history experienced in the First World War made a not inconsiderable contribution to the crisis.

The humanities changed from historical to hermeneutical disciplines, and here especially the name of Wilhelm Dilthey (1833-1911) should be mentioned. Their aim now lay no longer in explaining historical connections, but in understanding individual historical phenomena from themselves (see 3.4.3). Here the primary subject-matter was not historical events and those involved in them, but texts and works of art. Nor was there any particular interest either in the way in which these works were related to the personal life of their creators or in possible sources and models which had been used. Interest, rather, was in the work itself as the expression of a context in life. Philosophy now changed from being the history of philosophy into a philosophizing with the help of old texts, and literary criticism turned from the history of literature to 'text-immanent interpretation'.

This change and its significance for exegesis emerge in the third part of this book, not only in the specific discussion of 'hermeneutics' but also in the new exegetical approach of dialectical theology and the exegetical questions which went with it, in form criticism and in redaction criticism. Here too interpretation was more than an alternative to the natural sciences in the dispute over Darwinism; the biblical creation narrative was no longer to be read with the question whether it was historically correct but as a historical text which attempts to order the experienced reality of the world at a pre-scientific level.

In this form, too, the humanities are essentially related to history and investigate what in history is valid for the present. This value proves not least to be an aesthetic one. The term 'science' manifestly disappeared increasingly from descriptions and was surrendered to the natural sciences (in the media they alone are called 'science', and the humanities are referred to as 'culture'; so too is theology, when it is not classified under 'church'). That does not mean that there was a concern to be 'unscientific'; on the contrary, in the humanities there was a sense of superiority to 'pure' science, because their concern was not with dead matter but with living associations.

The humanities as a whole found themselves in a crisis because disciplines developed out of them which were also concerned with living contexts, but did not have a primarily historical or hermeneutical orientation. In particular these were psychology and sociology: here psychology was now no longer a description of the development of personality nor sociology a description of the structures of historical societies. Both, especially psychology, associated with the name of Sigmund Freud, found it difficult to gain a footing among the scientific discplines; sociology was more successful in so far as with Max Weber it represented itself as a historical discipline. With its search for rules and the connection between cause and effect it found itself methodologically closer to the natural sciences, but as the latent conflict between psychology and medicine shows, it did not find a home there either.

Their beginnings go back to the time of the controversy with historicism. In the meantime they have largely taken the lead in the humanities; in many places philosophy is changing once again from the history of philosophy, through a philosophical-type reflection on ancient texts, to an analysis of contemporary society; literary criticism is largely moving from the history of literature via text-immanent interpretation to the sociology of literature and above all to linguistics, which in turn is influenced, like psychology, by sociology. The methodological presupposition is no longer that the present can be understood in terms of the past but that it is understood in terms of itself. Here there is a heightened reflection of the insight that one cannot learn from history, and along with it the experience that today's world has finally proved to be so different from the past that it is virtually impossible to build a bridge of understanding to the past.

Theology, too, is involved in this change. The nature of theology has become more of a problem than in previous decades and there is also reflection on it as a theoretical problem. Theology once had to engage in discussion with scientific conceptuality which denied it the character of an academic discipline and thus its place within the university; now it is again being asked questions about its subject-matter and its methods. This change can be studied in discussions about the reform of theological study, which began with the alternatives 'empirical-critical'/ 'historical-critical', and thus with the question how theology should be defined as a whole, whether as a hermeneutical discipline or as the theory of church praxis.

M.F.Wiles, *What is Theology?*, Oxford University Press 1976;
E.Farley, *Theologia*, Fortress Press 1983;
J.Stacey, *Groundwork of Theology*, Epworth Press ²1984;
J.L.Houlden, *Connections*, SCM Press 1986.

1.3.3   The crisis in New Testament exegesis

Within theology, what used to be its leading discipline, New Testament exegesis, is most affected by this change. Both in study courses and in the interests of church organizations it has been moved from its key position to the periphery. Since it is so attached to historical criticism (rather than criticism of the present) and hermeneutical understanding (rather than change) few questions are now asked about it, or it is recognized only in a purified form (it is almost impossible now to use New Testament exegesis – in contrast to Old Testament exegesis – for writing sermon meditations; at most it helps with the 'preliminaries', i.e. 'just' exegesis).

So here the crisis of theology generally is at its clearest. We can see this crisis simply by putting a variety of positions side by side:

- The hermeneutical model has been summarized by G.Ebeling, *The Study of Theology*, Collins 1979. Here the New Testament, with the Old Testament subordinated to it, is the starting point of theology and its constant point of reference. Church history shows the communication of these texts as the history of the interpretation of the New Testament (and the Old). Systematic theology is the summarizing of the norms for Christianity which are contained in the New Testament; practical theology (primarily as homiletics and catechetics) is its communication to the present. In addition there is 'fundamental theology', which is a summary of this process of understanding, orientated wholly on the New Testament.

- In W.Pannenberg, *Theology and the Philosophy of Science*, Darton, Longman and Todd and Westminster Press 1974, the subject of theology is defined as 'religion' understood as a universal anthropological phenomenon. Thus Christian theology is the special instance of this universal religious discipline and exegesis, finally, is the account of the historical beginnings of this special instance. Here Pannenberg, following Gerhard von Rad, sees a special history of tradition leading from the Old Testament to the New. Thus exegesis, too, is just the study of the beginning of that religion which lies closest to us culturally, and which is exemplary for religion generally.

- Starting with the concept of 'critical theory', G.Petzke ('Exegese und Praxis', *Theologie und Praxis* 10, 1975, 2-19) defines the task of theology as criticism of the tradition with the aim of arriving at new norms through independent discussion. The aim of exegesis of the New Testament is to identify the origins of evils in our present society and thus overcome them.

- According to E.Güttgemanns (*Studia linguistica neotestamentica*, Beihefte zur Evangelischen Theologie 60, 1971), theology and thus exegesis can only claim to be scientific in so far as they present themselves as a linguistic discipline within the framework of linguistic study generally.

- The sociological question appears as the question of social history (thus especially G.Theissen, e.g. *The Social Setting of Pauline Christianity*, Fortress Press and T.& T.Clark 1981), as materialistic exegesis (thus e.g. in *Der Gott der kleinen Leute*, ed. W.Schottroff and W.Stegemann, 1979), or – particularly in the United States – in the adoption of sociological models to explain the phenomenon of 'early Christianity' (see Howard C.Kee, *Christian Origins in Sociological*

Perspective, SCM Press and Westminster Press 1980; Wayne A.Meeks, *The First Urban Christians*, Yale University Press 1984).

– Psychological approaches have been adopted in interpretations of texts (cf. the two collections edited by Y.Spiegel, *Psychoanalytische Interpretationen biblischer Texte* (1972) and *Doppeldeutlich. Tiefendimensionen biblischer Texte* (1978), but above all in a fundamentally different way of dealing with the texts – as being no longer historical but parts of one's one experience (cf. W.Wink, *Transforming Bible Study*, Abingdon Press and SCM Press 1981).

– P.Stuhlmacher (*Vom Verstehen des Neuen Testaments*, Grundrisse zum Neuen Testament 6, 1979) calls for a post-critical exegesis, the basis of which is to be an 'understanding with the text'; this comes about when the exegete surrenders his or her basically sceptical attitude and presupposes that New Testament texts are fundamentally correct in historical terms, thus providing historical verification for theological statements.

Such a survey of present trends and interests shows us how unclear the basic exegetical question 'What does the text say to me?' is at the present time. It is not only put in different ways, but is also defined with a solemnity which largely excludes other approaches, so that the individual positions do not just supplement or correct one another but are presented as alternatives to others (which are deemed to be 'false').

1.3.4   A study book on the New Testament

In view of this situation, a study book on the New Testament cannot be a summary of present New Testament scholarship. Nor, as a study book, can it be a one-sided account of a particular position within the broad spectrum of present possibilities, although it will inevitably have this character because it is in a particular tradition and does not set out to be an alternative to it.

One might cautiously describe this tradition as one which understands the texts of the New Testament as historical texts which are fundamental to the identity of theology and the church. So within theological disciplines it does not seem possible to define this identity on another basis. For New Testament scholarship itself, that means that as exegesis it has to do with texts and with history.

While there might be fairly broad agreement on defining the task in this way, the present book now emphatically takes up the history of the interpretation of the New Testament, especially since the rise of the modern historical consciousness, and attempts to present what this history shows to be possible (and impossible). It does not give alternatives to historical-critical and theological exegesis, but takes up questions from there which still seem to be significant today.

Underlying the book is a certain mistrust of 'methods'. I have replaced this term throughout by 'questions'; by this I mean sets of questions which arise from reading the New Testament texts themselves, but which as such also correspond to universal questions of a particular time. Here a circle between the text and the situation of the interpreter emerges which is constantly broken, only to be re-formed once more.

So these exegetical questions are not simply individual questions that can be added up, posed independently of one another and lead to results which can be brought together; as will emerge, at least part of the time they compete with one another. Therefore there is no such thing as 'the historical-critical method', or rather, there is no longer such a thing, if by that one means the historical theology in a strict sense which is described in the second part of this book. When we take up old questions nowadays, we no longer do so in the sense in which they were originally intended.

The individual sections which deal with these exegetical questions are constructed in the following way. First the basic problem is indicated. Then follow accounts of the history of the particular problem and of various attempts at a solution which have been offered in this history. Then in the last part a defining question is formulated to match the relevant set of questions. This defining question always formalizes or even neutralizes the original concern; it may, for example, give a survey of possibilities of gaining insight into individual areas of the New Testament text by the use of the question.

The division of the book into two main sections, 'historical theology' and 'theological exegesis', stems from the history of theology and the history of New Testament study which corresponds to it; the individual complexes of exegetical questions are raised in their context in the history of theology. It is impossible to find such a historical setting for the 'further questions' discussed in the fourth part, which arise out of the latest change in the humanities. They can only indicate current problems for exegesis which have yet to be formalized in a methodical way.

Finally, this book is based on a particular understanding of study as a way of enabling the student to make his or her own responsible judgments. The definition of this aim is hardly likely to be controversial. But I have drawn from it the conclusion that in this kind of book the pattern of giving and receiving information which is usual elsewhere should be avoided. Certainly the broadest possible information is needed for forming judgments, and this too is given in the book; but study must be more than taking in and understanding such information and learning formal possibilities, and in my view account must be taken of this on the very first encounter with this information.

This book has come into being from notes for introductory courses which have been worked over again and again since 1965 – in Heidelberg, Bethel and now in Marburg. Those who have taken part in these courses have often felt over-stretched; where I saw such complaints as being merely a desire for 'correct information' I have not departed from my aim. In the introductory courses the notes were linked with particular tasks which were carried out before coming to the defining questions. So the process was a matter of beginning from the individual phenomena of a particular text and only then generalizing in a methodical way from the questions which arose; in educational terms the approach was therefore inductive, not deductive. That, too, is meant to avoid the pattern of giving and receiving information. However, the conditions of an introductory course of this kind cannot be reproduced in a book, and the book is not meant to replace the introductory course, even if it could.

So as a study book this book seeks not so much to teach as to make the reader think. The bibliographies are intended neither to intimidate readers nor to give them a bad conscience. What I would prefer to do here is to give some pointers which may or may not be of interest in connection with a particular problem, so that those who are interested and want to know more on a particular subject can find it.

The aim of the book is to make the material as elementary as possible – some extremely complicated passages will show that this does not mean simplification. Making the material elementary has also meant putting the section on the texts right at the beginning (1.2); this offers an incentive to engage in some elementary exegesis from which the specialized questions then arise. Without being committed to a linguistic programme and without adopting any special technical terms from one, this first part is a free appropriation of observations derived from one.

At first, exegesis makes the texts seem strange; as long as this effect of alienation is not artificially induced by means of a method, but helps to bring out what is strange in the texts and does not allow them to go over into what is in any case familiar, exegesis as such is finally a theological programme. This programme involves not just measuring the texts by one's own questions but also listening to the questions raised by the texts themselves, whether they now seem appropriate or not.

1.3.5   Secondary literature

In principle you should work on exegesis as long as possible without secondary literature, and instead first come to grips with the text in the elementary way indicated in 1.2, before going on to raise the particular exegetical questions which will be mentioned later. Only then should you turn to the secondary literature, to look there for possible ways of solving the questions which arise from this work. Perhaps you will also come up against other perspectives which you might have overlooked. Such a mode of working will help to avoid the effect that from the beginning you read the text under the spell of a particular given exegesis and then have no criteria for assessing another divergent exegesis. When dealing with secondary literature it is worth noting the positions of particular authors and the kind of arguments with which they support their own positions and reject those of others. This is the only way of judging a position, and a comparison between comments on a topic from different authors must take into account the basis from which they argue. (It is always advisable to mistrust arguments which are supposed to be 'natural' or 'clear'; nor should one be intimidated by appeals to authorities which are alleged to have demonstrated something conclusively.) Here too the aim is to achieve an independent and responsible judgment in accepting or rejecting the views you encounter in the secondary literature.

The basic literature first includes books entitled *Introduction to the New Testament*, etc. These discuss the content of individual books of the New Testament and the circumstances of their composition (author, sources, time, audience). Their accounts should not, however, be taken as objective descriptions; it is always necessary to remember that their authors have no different sources of information from ours, i.e. primarily the texts, and that they are arguing on the basis of these texts. For example, how the opponents of Paul in a particular letter are to be defined depends on the interpretation of the letter as a whole:

R.M.Grant, *A Historical Introduction to the New Testament*, Collins 1963;
W.Marxsen, *Introduction to the New Testament*, Blackwell 1968;
W.G.Kümmel, *Introduction to the New Testament*, SCM Press and Abingdon Press 1975;
R.F.Collins, *Introduction to the New Testament*, Doubleday and SCM Press 1983;
Luke T.Johnson, *The Writings of the New Testament*, Fortress Press and SCM Press 1986.

Books entitled *Theology of the New Testament*, etc. summarize the theology of the individual writings or groups of writings (Paul, John) in the New Testament. In principle these should be dealt with in the same way as the Introductions.

R.Bultmann, *Theology of the New Testament* (two volumes), SCM Press and Scribner 1953, 1955;
J.Jeremias, *New Testament Theology* I, *The Proclamation of Jesus*, SCM Press and Scribner 1971;
L.Goppelt, *Theology of the New Testament* (two volumes), Eerdmans 1981, 1982.

For the theology of Paul see H.-J.Schoeps, *Paul*, Lutterworth Press 1961;
H.Ridderbos, *Paul*, SPCK 1977;
J.C.Beker, *Paul the Apostle*, Fortress Press and T.& T.Clark 1980.

For Johannine theology see C.H.Dodd, *The Interpretation of the Fourth Gospel*, Cambridge University Press 1953;
E.Käsemann, *The Testament of Jesus*, SCM Press and Fortress Press 1968.

There are various commentary series, more or less complete, which cover all the New Testament books paragraph by paragraph, and indeed often verse by verse:

Hermeneia (Fortress Press) presupposes specialist knowledge; less demanding are the SCM Press/Penguin New Testament Commentaries, the New Century Bible (Oliphants); Word Commentaries (Word Publishing Company, Waco, Texas); the Anchor Bible (Doubleday); and the Black/Harper New Testament Commentaries (which appear under the name of their respective publishers Harper and Row in the US and A. & C.Black in Britain).

The most important journals relating to the New Testament are:

JBL	*Journal of Biblical Literature*
NTS	*New Testament Studies*
NT	*Novum Testamentum*
ZNW	*Zeitschrift für die neutestamentliche Wissenschaft und die Kunde der älteren Kirche*
BZ	*Biblische Zeitschrift*
Bib	*Biblica*

Monographs are books in which a more or less extensive special topic is discussed. Important series for New Testament exegesis, many of which are cited in this volume, are:

ATANT	Abhandlungen zur Theologie des Alten und Neuen Testaments
FRLANT	Forschungen zur Religion und Literatur des Alten und Neuen Testaments
WMANT	Wissenschaftliche Monographien zum Alten und Neuen Testament
SANT	Studien zum Alten und Neuen Testament
SNT	Studien zum Neuen Testament

NTA	Neutestamentliche Abhandlungen
SBT	Studies in Biblical Theology
SNTS.M	Society of·New Testament Studies Monographs (Cambridge University Press)
JSNT.SS	Journal for the Study of the New Testament, Supplement Series (Sheffield)
SNTW	Studies of the New Testament and its World

There are bibliographical journals which list all the scholarly literature on the NT (OT and Judaism) which has appeared in a particular year; this is classified both in the order of the New Testament writings and from thematic perspectives:

For the English-speaking world see especially *New Testament Abstracts*, published in the United States.

Theological lexicons also contain special articles on questions of introduction and theology:

X.Léon-Dufour, *Dictionary of Biblical Theology*, Geoffrey Chapman 1973;
E.Livingstone (ed.), *Oxford Dictionary of the Christian Church*, Oxford University Press ²1974;
The Interpreter's Dictionary of the Bible, Abingdon Press 1962ff. (four volumes and a supplementary volume).

2.1   The question of the original text: textual criticism

2.1.1   The basic problem

The basic problem of textual criticism is that we do not have the original of any New Testament writing – though the same is true of Old Testament writings and of writings from antiquity generally. What we have are copies of copies; in the case of the New Testament the earliest come from the second and third centuries, and the bulk of them from the Middle Ages. There are an amazing number: more than 5000 Greek manuscripts with text from the New Testament are known, and in addition to this there are early translations, whereas in the case of many ancient authors scholars are glad if even a single manuscript has been preserved in the original and they are not just dependent on translations.

The tradition is clearly quite different even with the 'Apostolic Fathers' (see 1.1.5): for example, there is only one complete manuscript of the Didache in Greek (dated 1056), while others of these works (Letter of Barnabas, I and II Clement) have a better tradition only because they occur in manuscripts of the New Testament (Barnabas in Sinaiticus, I and II Clement in Alexandrinus).

B.Metzger, *The Text of the New Testament*, Oxford 1964;

K. and B.Aland, *The Text of the New Testament*, Eerdmans 1987.

2.1.2   The writing down and muliplication of texts

We learn only by chance about the writing down of New Testament texts, from the texts themselves. Thus in Rom.16.22 a Tertius who has written the letter at Paul's dictation sends his greetings; Paul adds a conclusion in his own hand in 6.11-18 to the Letter to the Galatians (cf. the greeting in his own hand in I Cor.16.21), while he wrote the short letter to Philemon completely by himself (v.19). From our knowledge

of contemporary ways of producing Greek literature we can conclude
that the New Testament writings were from the start written on
individual pages which could be joined together, not on extended scrolls
like the writings of the Old Testament (cf. above all the Qumran scrolls),
and in capitals, so-called majuscules. Before the invention of printing,
the multiplication of texts was possible only by copying from a model,
either directly or through dictation. (It was photography which first
made possible the reproduction of original handwriting without setting
it in print.)

Many later copies contain precise information about the scribe and
the place and date of the copy. Otherwise dating is possible only by the
style of writing, which changes over the course of time, and by the
material; that is the explanation of how indications of age can be given
for individual manuscripts.

The simplest writing material was papyrus sheets, which were made
by cutting and sticking together the stems of papyrus plants. These
papyrus plants grow mainly, but not exclusively, in Egypt. The dry
leaves are very sensitive to moisture, and so they have been preserved
almost only in the dry desert sand of Egypt. Such leaves are referred to
as papyrus, plural papyri, hence the English word paper. So far 88 such
papyri are known for the textual tradition of the New Testament, from
small scraps (p^{52}) to relatively extensive books (p^{46}, the oldest, almost
complete, manuscript of the letters of Paul). As papyri mostly date
from between the second and fourth centuries and thus are older than
most other manuscripts, they are important for the textual tradition of
the New Testament, and particular note is made of them in editions of
the New Testament text. The writing on them is majuscule (capitals).
They are denoted by a p (= papyrus) with consecutive superior numbers
(e.g. p^{52} or p^{46}).

Parchment, made from animal skin, was much more durable as a
writing material, but also much more expensive. The city of Pergamon
in western Asia Minor was pre-eminent in making it, hence the
name. Anyone who had writing done on parchment attached special
importance to what was written and wanted a permanent record. For
the New Testament we know such parchment manuscripts from the
fourth century; it is probably no coincidence that this is the time when
Christianity became the official religion of the Roman empire under
the emperor Constantine. Now there are books (for which the Latin
word is *codex*, plural *codices*) which contain (or, where we only have
fragments, will once have contained) either the whole of the New (and
Old) Testament largely in its present extent (see above, 1.1.3) or parts
of it (Gospels or letters of Paul, etc.).

The writing continues to be majuscule, sometimes already with reading and punctuation marks, above all in cases of doubt. But from the ninth century there begins the change to the small letters (minuscules) with which we are familiar. As a technical term 'majuscule' denotes not only the form of writing but in particular also parchment manuscripts with capitals; another term for them is 'uncials' (from 'inch', as the length of the letters). These were originally denoted by capitals: A,B,C, etc.; when the Latin alphabet ran out they were then denoted by Greek characters and finally also by Hebrew characters, e.g. ℵ. ℵ was used because the man who discovered the manuscript which it denotes, Tischendorf (see 2.1.4 below), thought that this first of all letters would give it a status above all others. The disadvantage of this kind of designation is that the same letter came to be used to denote two or even three different codices, depending on their content. So a second way of enumerating them, with Arabic figures after a prefixed 0, is safer: e.g. ℵ = 01, A = 02, H for the Gospels = 013, for Acts and the Catholic Epistles = 014, for the letters of Paul = 015. In total, the numbering of the majuscules has now reached 0277. However, it was later recognized that some of these were separated parts of a single manuscript; by contrast, 0212 is not a manuscript with a New Testament text.

Some of these majuscules were also named after the place in which they were found or preserved, or after their owner, and appear in the literature under this name. As these names are longer given in the 26th edition of Nestle-Aland, in contrast to earlier editions (and although knowledge of what they stand for is taken for granted in the introduction), here are the most important ones that the student should know:

ℵ (01) = Sinaiticus (after the place where it was found: St Catherine's monastery on Mt Sinai);
A (02) = Alexandrinus (from the library of the Patriarch of Alexandria; from the seventeenth century it has been in England);
B (03) = Vaticanus (in the Vatican library);
C (04) = Ephraemi rescriptus (originally a manuscript with a NT text which was later cleaned off so that the tractates of the Syrian church father Ephraem could be written on it – such a reused typescript is called a 'palimpsest');
D (05) = Bezae Cantabrigiensis (once in the possession of the reformer Theodor Beza, and kept in Cambridge), contains the Gospels, Acts and the Catholic Letters. It is to be distinguished from
D (06) = Claromontanus (after Clermont, where it used to be kept; it is now in Paris): contains the letters of Paul;
G (012) = Boernerianus (formerly in St Gallen, now in Dresden) contains the letters of Paul.

Minuscules are denoted with Arabic figures without a prefixed 0; the
number of them known to us is more than ten times as great as that of
the majuscules, because the minuscules only come from the Middle
Ages (nearer to the present day, and a wider circulation of biblical
manuscripts). They represent a uniform type of text, that customary in
the Greek church.

2.1.3   The Greek text in the West

The translation by the church father Jerome (who died in 420), the
Vulgate, became the usual text for the Latin-speaking West; it replaced
the various earlier Latin translations (Itala, or Old Latin). However, as
a consequence of humanism with its new interest in Greek and its
programme of a return to the original sources there was a new interest
in the West in the Greek text of the New Testament at the beginning of
the sixteenth century. The first edition, now in the form of a printed
book, was made in 1514 as part of an edition of the whole Bible in
several parallel columns in (Hebrew and Aramaic for the Old Testament
and in) Greek and Latin. This work was edited by the Spanish Cardinal
Ximenes and is called the 'Complutensian Polyglot': 'Complutensian'
after the Spanish city of Alcala (Latin *Complutum*), and 'polyglot'
because of its multiplicity of languages. Although it was finished in
1514, papal permission was only given for the New Testament volume
in 1520, and it probably came on to the market only in 1522.

Meanwhile, however, in 1516 an edition had appeared from the
printer Froben(ius) which was to have far more influence subsequently,
that by Erasmus of Rotterdam (1469-1536). Although the mass of
printing errors in the second edition which was called for as early as
1519 had been corrected by the fourth edition of 1527, this edition is of
relatively poor quality. The reason for this is that Erasmus based it only
on inferior manuscripts from the twelfth century; because there was no
Greek textual basis for the final verse of the Revelation of John, the
edition even had it in a retrotranslation from the Latin.

However, the influence of Erasmus' edition derives above all from
the fact that the second edition of 1519 was the textual basis for Luther's
1522 translation of the New Testament. Thus up to the revision of the
Luther text in 1956 the Erasmus text was binding as the extent and
textual form of the official German text of the New Testament. It was
not until 1975 that a revision put the Luther text on a new basis.

In the course of time, more and more Greek manuscripts became
known in the West and their readings were incorporated into the
Erasmus text in a manner which could only partially be checked. Thus

there came into being what was called the *textus receptus*, a term from
the publisher's advertising for an edition which appeared in 1633 from
the Elsevier brothers in Leiden. It was claimed that this edition was the
text which was now acknowledged by all (*textum ergo habes, nunc ab
omnibus receptum*), and in fact it became the basis for the English King
James Bible and for other Protestant translations of the Bible. It was
this text, too, which was regarded as the inspired wording in the later
doctrine of the literal communication of the Bible by God himself,
though this doctrine was developed against rising criticism of this edition
on the basis of newly discovered manuscripts.

The verse-divison with which we are familiar goes back to an edition
by the printer Stephanus which appeared in Geneva in 1551; the chapter
division was already being used in the Middle Ages.

2.1.4   The nineteenth century

Up to the beginning of the nineteenth century, textual criticism was
essentially limited to the collection of divergent readings, and attention
was paid above all to minuscules. Nevertheless as a result notice had
already been taken of the textual tradition at the end of the Gospel of
Mark (Mark 16.9-20) and of the pericope of the woman taken in adultery
(John 7.53-8.11). Two numbers show what the nineteenth century
meant: in 1806 only 481 Greek manuscripts could be listed as known;
by 1909 the figure was 4079. This progress resulted from the opening
up of the East to the West by the collapse of the Turkish Empire and
runs parallel to the development of archaeology in the nineteenth
century. It was furthered above all by the travels of individual scholars
who systematically searched through monastery libraries. The best
known of them is Constantine von Tischendorf (1815-1874), who
discovered in St Catherine's Monastery on Sinai among other works
the Codex Sinaiticus (‎א), so named after the place where it was found;
after a number of complications Tischendorf took it to St Petersburg,
present-day Leningrad, from where it was sold by the Soviet Govern-
ment to the British Museum in London in 1933 for the sum of £100,000.

Above all from his own manuscript discoveries Tischendorf produced
an edition of the text which was reprinted several times; the eighth
edition was published between 1869 and 1872 in Leipzig. In 1881, after
long preliminary work, B.F.Westcott and F.J.A.Hort produced their
The Greek New Testament in the Original Greek; they had not searched
for new manuscripts but relied on the information of others and on
collections of variants.

The progress in textual criticism during the nineteenth century consists in the way in which as a result of the discovery of manuscripts substantially different from the familiar *textus receptus* scholars came to distinguish an earlier type of text from a later one; the later one, above all represented in the mass of minuscules, went back to something like a revision at the time when the church, now officially recognized as a religion, needed uniform texts in many copies for the church buildings which were being constructed everywhere. The decisive step between the earlier and the later type of text was taken in the fourth century. The designations for these two types vary, and there is a large number of proposals for further sub-groupings. The following designations have become established: 𝕳 (a Gothic H) = 'Hesychian' (after a Hesychius who was supposed to be the editor) or 'Egyptian' (after the place of origin of the most important manuscripts of this group) text, represented above all by the great codexes ℵ, B,C, and apart from the Gospels also by A; 𝕶 (a Gothic K) = 'koine' text (after the Greek word for 'common'), the later text form (also imperial text or Byzantine text). Of the remaining designations for groups, only 'Western text' has really been maintained; this is represented above all by D in Acts.

2.1.5   'Nestle'

Novum Testamentum graece, edited by Eberard Nestle, appeared for the first time in 1898. In it the results of the textual criticism of the nineteenth century were worked out in a very simple but convincing way in a brief volume which was easy to use; since then it has had a very wide circulation and gone through many editions.

Nestle did not produce his text from the manuscripts himself, but from the printed editions by Tischendorf (T) and Westcott/Hort (H), along with that of R.F.Weymouth (1892), and he did so by a simple majority decision. The divergent versions of the other editors were noted in a first apparatus, and in a second a few divergent readings, but without any indication of the manuscripts from which they came. From the third edition (1901) onwards the edition by B.Weiss (= W, 1894/ 1900) replaced that of Weymouth in arriving at the majority; note had already been taken of it in the first edition. Primitive though this majority procedure may seem, it led to a good text compared with the *textus receptus*, which was still the text commonly used at that time, thanks to the fact that the editions by Tischendorf and Westcott/Hort were based on valuable manuscripts.

The second apparatus was extended up until the twelfth edition of 1923, and improved by also naming the manuscripts. From the thirteenth edition of 1927, now edited by Eberhard Nestle's son Erwin, both apparatuses were combined: first the divergent readings were noted, and then after a semicolon the editions were given, a pattern which is still familiar to those who use the twenty-fifth edition. Moreover from this thirteenth edition on, note was also taken of the 1913 edition of the NT by Hermann von Soden. From the seventeenth edition of 1941 there were also occasional departures from the majority principle.

From the twenty-first edition of 1952 onwards, Kurt Aland became the editor of 'Nestle'. Above all after the foundation of the Institute for New Testament Textual Research at Münster under his direction in 1959 the readings were no longer taken from the printed editions but checked from the manuscripts themselves and then incorporated into the editions up to the twenty-fifth. At the same time, the twenty-sixth edition, which has now been been available since 1979, was prepared (= N^{26}). This finally took leave of the majority principle which had still been influential up to the twenty-fifth edition and prepared the apparatus only from manuscripts (the information about the different nineteenth- and twentieth-century editions of the text can be found in an appendix on pp.717-38).

At the same time this work was put in an international and ecumenical context which resulted in *The Greek New Testament* (= GNT) which has been taken over by a variety of Bible Societies. This first appeared in 1966 (edited by K.Aland, M.Black, B.M.Metzger and A.Wikgren), and finally in a third edition in 1975, now with the collaboration of the Catholic C.M.Martini (= GNT[3]). The body of the text in GNT[3] corresponds with N^{26} (though there are differences in proper names and in the punctuation), and the commentary by Bruce Metzger which goes with it gives the reasons for the most important text-critical decisions.

B.M.Metzger, *A Textual Commentary on the Greek New Testament*, 1971

The aim of GNT was to secure a common Greek textual basis for Bible translations into all languages (it was used as the basis for the revision of the Luther Bible in 1975). This revision proved controversial because it departed from familiar phrases in the Luther text, and also because some verses were omitted for text-critical considerations (e.g. Mark 7.16). In practice, then, one encounters the problem of textual criticism when comparing the new text of the Luther Bible (and indeed that of other moden translations) with the Old. Progress can be seen above all in the fact that now, for the first time since the depature from the *textus receptus*, the Greek text with which theologians work agrees in extent and form with the official text which is used in the church.

In the text itself, apart from the new type-face, the differences between N^{26} and N^{25} are not very great; the quality of the previous

Nestle is confirmed. The text-critical signs have also remained the same. On the other hand, the apparatus under the text has been given a fundamentally new look. As I have already mentioned, references to the editions have disappeared. The main new feature is the omission of the collective designations 𝕳 and 𝕶 which were used until N25, and in many cases it is clear how misleading the simple identification 𝕳 = older, better; 𝕶 = younger, worse could be.

They have been replaced by a listing of the manuscripts. Because it is impossible to give a complete list of all the manuscripts in a small handy edition (a large edition in fifteen volumes is planned), a selection and qualitative evaluation is made using the concept of 'continuous witnesses' (cf. N26 11*-17*). There is a first category of these which is redefined in every book of the New Testament, manuscripts which are mentioned in each instance; from this it is possible to conclude that if these manuscripts are not cited they do not contain the passage in question. These are (almost) all the papyri, the old majuscules and a few minuscules (for e.g. Romans see N26 14* middle). In addition there are secondary continuous witnesses, each of which is always noted for a group of writings (Gospels, Acts, letters of Paul: p.15* middle; Catholic letters, Revelation). A new sign, 𝔐 (M written in Gothic), is introduced in connection with this second group; despite its similarity to the earlier signs 𝕳 and 𝕶, this does not denote a fixed group of manuscripts but is a neutral designation for 'majority of Greek manuscripts' ('majority text'). In fact the 'majority text' is what used to be called the Koine, if we note from N26, 711, the mass of minuscules which the editors assign to 𝔐.

In work with the text-critical apparatus 𝔐 primarily has the function of being an abbreviation for a carefully defined number of manscripts, each of which has to be redefined at each passage. It occurs only (but cf. Mark 13.2; Luke 6.25) where there is mention not only of readings which diverge from the text offered and the manuscripts which attest them but also (after *txt*) as attestation for the text put forward by the editor. The manuscripts which are subsumed under 𝔐 in any particular case can be seen from the following procedure:

First take the list of secondary 'continuous witnesses' which relate to the passage in question (the 'continuous witnesses' in the first category must in any case be cited individually where they contain the text), and delete the manuscripts which are mentioned as support for another reading. Then make sure by means of the extents of the remaining manuscripts listed in Appendix I (684-710) which of them in fact contains the passage in question. The manscripts still left are 𝔐 in this particular instance; however, if one takes p.711 into account, this is at the same time a qualitative judgment. The introduction of this abbreviation provides a considerable amount of information; using this procedure certainly takes more time than using the earlier editions of Nestle, but it leads to more precise results. Anyone in search of more precise information on the individual manuscripts than appears in Appendix I (which unfortunately does not even contain the names of the great codexes) should consult in addition to the books mentioned at 2.1.1 above:

P.R.Ackroyd and C.F.Evans (eds.), *The Cambridge History of the Bible*, Vol.1, Cambridge University Press 1970 (Chapter 11, by J.N.Birdsall).

The apparatus of GNT[3] looks very different. It is dictated by the purpose of this edition (which is to provide a basic text for translations of the Bible and takes into account textual variants which underlie existing translations. With GNT[3] or N[26] a form of the text seems to have been achieved which may be regarded as something like a standard text for a long time. Accordingly, textual criticism plays a much smaller role in the exegesis of the New Testament than in the Old (and also in the discussion of texts from church history). Even in the new *Biblia Hebraica Stuttgartensia*, the usual text of the Hebrew Old Testament is the reprint of a single manuscript, the Codex Leningradensis (L). The apparatus mentions readings in other manuscripts which differ from it, and also translations which suggest a divergent basic Hebrew text, and it contains suggestions from the editors as to how a more correct reading of the text might be achieved. Here, then, in weighing up the information and the proposals in the apparatus one first has to discover the text on which one wants to base the exegesis.

By contrast GNT[3] or N[26] (like their predecessors) are partly reconstructed texts which do not correspond as a whole to any of the manuscripts; accordingly, the proposals from the editors about readings are not in the apparatus but in the text itself. So here a personal decision is largely dispensed with; however, such a decision is necessary in the very frequent instances in which the editors have put parts of the text in square brackets, i.e. where in their view it is not clear what belongs to the original text. It is also necessary where in the Gospels Greeven's synopsis (see 2.2.4) suggests a different text from GNT[3] or N[26].

2.1.6　　　Textual criticism as exegetical questioning

The defining question for textual criticism is: What was the text originally written by the author of the work in question?

Given differing readings in the manuscripts, the basic principle for making a decision in textual criticism lies in the question: Which reading is best explained as an alteration of the others?

Some remarks which supplement one another may be of further help here:

– The more difficult reading (*lectio difficilior*) is usually the better one, on the principle that a copyist wants to simplify a text rather than make it more difficult.
– The shorter reading (*lectio brevior*) is as a rule the better one, on the principle that the copyist is more likely to explain a difficult text by additions than to abbreviate it.
– Earlier manuscripts are usually better witnesses, but mistakes may already have crept in at a very early stage in some strands of the textual tradition (for example, although p[46] is the earliest mansucript of the letters of Paul, it is by no means always the one whose reading has been adopted in N[26]).
– In the case of the Gospels (and also elsewhere), as a rule the better reading is the one which diverges from a parallel text in the other Gospels, on the principle that a copyist is more likely to assimilate to a parallel text than to depart from it.
– You can study the sources of mistakes by copying out favourite texts yourself. For example omissions can be caused by the eye confusing its last point of reference with a similar word further down the text when one has looked away briefly. Mistakes can also happen in the change from one kind of writing into another, in the case of the New Testament tradition above all in the transition from majuscules to minuscules. But mistakes can also appear when a copyist thinks that the text in front of him cannot be right and seeks to improve its content, in this case above all for dogmatic reasons.
– In view of the large number of Greek manuscripts in existence, the translations play only a small role. For the same reason it is hard to make out a case for 'conjectures', i.e. proposals by editors and commentators which are not attested in any manuscript, although they are still mentioned relatively frequently in N[26].
– K. and B.Aland (*Text*, 167-79) have graded the individual Greek manuscripts. They arrange them into five categories, of which categories I and II roughly correspond to the former 𝔓, and category V to 𝔐, while the manuscripts of the 'Western' text belong to category IV. Such a classification has to be taken into account in any text-critical decision, because as a rule one begins from the assumption that in individual instances, also, a 'better' manuscript will have a better text. In no way can the majority of manuscripts be decisive because, as this table shows, the majority belong in the worse category.
– In addition to its strictly text-critical function of determining the

original text, by indicating differences, even if they are irrelevant to establishing the original text, an apparatus can indicate particular difficulties in the traditional text. For example, the manuscripts often show signs of interpretations and clarifications of ambiguous passages; this is particularly striking in the case of the 'Western' text of Acts.

Text-critical problems on a larger scale can be found at the end of the Gospel of Mark (after 16.8); in the passage about 'the woman taken in adultery' which appears in most manuscripts as John 7.53-8.11; and at the end of Romans (after 16.23) (for details see commentaries on the books concerned).

The *Comma Johanneum* has played a role in the history of dogma; this is a variant to I John 5.7f. which appears in a few late Greek manuscripts and above all in the Latin translation. That was because it would be one of two explicit points of reference for the Christian doctrine of the Trinity in the New Testament.

The discovery that according to the better witnesses I Tim.3.16 does not begin with the Greek word for God (thus Luther's translation 'God is revealed in the flesh') but with the masculine relative pronoun, which does not agree with the noun in the neuter ('mystery') which precedes it, had similar significance. This passage would be one of the very few in the New Testament in which Christ was designated God along the lines of christological dogma. The variant has arisen first from the offence taken to the grammar (other manuscripts put the relative pronoun in the neuter) and then from a concern for dogmatic correctness; *theos* and *hos* would in any case be easy to confuse, as some sacred words were written in abbreviated form in Greek manuscripts; in majuscule writing *theos* appeared as HC, and OC, *hos*, was easy to confuse with it.

On the other hand, despite the less good attestation one must read the indicative in Rom.5.1, as the subjunctive simply would not fit Paul's theology.

2.2   The question of the original sources: literary criticism

2.2.1   The basic problem

In the case of narrative texts the basic problem of literary criticism proves to be the simple question where the author gets what he writes from. However, this question only becomes a matter of principle when one is strictly asking about the human authors in the Bible and puts into the background the theory of mediated or even direct authorship by the

Holy Spirit which is developed in the doctrine of inspiration. None of the authors of the narrative books in fact refers to such legitimation; the Third Evangelist, who is the only one to give us any account of his way of working, refers to books which had already been written (Luke 1.1-4). Nor do any of the narrators claim to be eyewitnesses of what they report; in John 21.24, the second conclusion to the Fourth Gospel, following 20.30f. (see 2.2.5), the author is identified with the Beloved Disciple – by others. Gospels which claim to be based on direct eyewitness, like the Gospel of Peter, appear among the apocryphal Gospels.

2.2.2   The juxtaposition of different kinds of texts

For narrative texts (Gospels, Acts) the literary-critical question is the question what sources underlie them. While this question is simple to answer in the case of Gal.1.13-2.21, where Paul is reporting his own experience, when we consider the part of Acts (9-15) which covers the same period of time we have to ask where Luke got his information from; he is reporting in the past tense and some time afterwards, without mentioning any sources. Not inconsiderable differences between Paul and Luke (e.g. the journey in Acts 11.29f.; 12.25 which cannot be reconciled with Gal.1.13-2.21) seem to rule out the possibiity that Luke used the letters of Paul as sources, especially as he does not mention such letters anywhere.

Right from the beginning, the fact that there was more than one Gospel caused a problem (1.13); instead of one Gospel, there were four of them in the canon. Here, too, the not inconsiderable differences in the account led (and continue to lead) to harmonizations: either the different accounts were just added together, or contradictions were removed by a tacit decision in favour of one of the accounts. We can see the problem from the question what Jesus's last words were before his death, Matt.27.46, Mark 15.34, Luke 23.46 or John 19.30 (the church tradition has harmonized them into the 'seven last words from the cross'), or from the question whether the Friday on which Jesus was crucified was the first day of the feast of the passover (see Matt.26.17; Mark 14.12; Luke 22.7) or the day before (thus John 18.28; 19.14,31).

Such observations were of no theological significance as long as one held to the traditional dogma, if one wanted to know who Jesus 'really was'. The Jesus of the Gospel of John corresponded most closely to christological dogma, and Luther still valued the Fourth Gospel more highly than the first three, because one could learn more from it about Jesus' relationship with God. At the same time there was an awareness that the first three belong very closely together. They sometimes correspond even down to the wording of whole sentences; have a largely common structure; and in comparison with the Gospel of John, Jesus talks about himself in them very rarely. The Gospel of John itself is characterized by Jesus' long discourses about his task as the Son of the Father sent into the world; in this Gospel Jesus goes up to the feast of the passover in Jerusalem three times, and not just once to his passion. Moreover, where it contains stories which appear in the other three Gospels it differs much more widely from them than they do from one another.

2.2.3   The nineteenth century

The relationship between the four Gospels became a topic of discussion from the eighteenth century on. But it became a theological problem in the historical theology of the nineteenth century, which could no longer accept an answer to the question who Jesus 'really was' in terms of traditional dogma, but could only put it as a historical question and look for historical verification.

W.R.Farmer, *The Synoptic Problem*, Macmillan, New York 1964;
C.Tuckett, *Reading the New Testament*, SPCK 1987.

Theology allied itself with the historicism of the historical sciences generally, a historicism which developed as a scientific method both over against the traditional picture of history and its 'legends' and against the speculation of German idealism and its philosophy of history. The question 'how it really happened' was to be answered 'only from the sources'; here it was a matter of evaluating and weighing up the individual sources. So the nineteenth century saw an enormous increase in the critical editions of texts, including work on the original text of the New Testament (see 2.1.4); the prerequisite for this work was the systematic investigation of old libraries and archives.

The concept of truth underlying this understanding of history is that of historical truth as opposed to legend; that is true which can be demonstrated by historical method. Only what is historically real is true, and conversely, only what can be proved to be true by historical study is real. This legacy has determined our understanding of reality to the present day, and still plays a role in discussions about the reliability of the Bible, when 'reliability' means 'did it really happen or not?'.

David Friedrich Strauss (1808-1874) and his book *The Life of Jesus Critically Examined* (1835) proved particularly oppressive for theology. By radicalizing the philosophy of Hegel, Strauss understood Jesus as the embodiment of the idea of the God-man and the New Testament accounts of Jesus as myth, which really spoke of the human race as a whole.

See David Friedrich Strauss, *The Life of Jesus Critically Examined*, translated by George Eliot, reissued Fortress Press and SCM Press 1972;
Horton Harris, *David Friedrich Strauss and his Theology*, Cambridge University Press 1974;
W.G.Kümmel, *The New Testament. The History of the Investigation of its Problems*, Nashville and London 1973, 120-8.

The controversy with Strauss shaped New Testament scholarship for many decades and led to historical-critical exegesis in the strict sense. One can see this change from the difference in value judgments associated with two words: whereas for the idealistic philosophy of history the appropriate method was 'speculation' and the concern was to recognize the 'idea' in the chances of history, there could now be no worse charge against a historian than the production of '(pure) speculation' and '(mere) idea'. At the same time this finally led to the criticism of dogma, which had shaped study of the New Testament, especially since the Enlightenment. To this degree historical criticism is more than mere method; it is part of the history of theology in German Protestantism (see 2.4).

2.2.4   The synoptic problem

To combat Strauss, a historical picture of the man Jesus of Nazareth had to be secured. For this, reliable sources were needed, and this meant a clarification of the relationship between the four Gospels. The close affinity in content of the first three Gospels in comparison with the fourth allowed a choice to be made between the former and the latter; the decision went in favour of the simpler three as opposed to the 'speculative' Gospel of John, which moreover was sometimes dated extremely late – even to the end of the second century (the publication in 1935 of p⁵², which contains part of the Gospel of John, finally put an end to such late datings, as this papyrus was written around 125 and the Gospel of John must therefore have been written before that).

The comprehensive term for the first three Gospels was 'synoptic' (from the Greek *synopsis* = see together). The relationship between them had to be clarified: this is the 'synoptic problem'. Preliminary work on this went back into the eighteenth century. In principle we have to distinguish two types of model here; the first presupposes a kind of primal Gospel behind the Gospels as we now have them, on which the evangelists drew, each for himself and independently of one another. The second model conjectures a dependence on the evangelists on one another and thus a historical sequence between the Gospels.

The first model was used in the following proposed solutions:
- by G.E.Lessing (1729-1781) in the 'primal Gospel hypothesis': a Gospel which has not been preserved, but which can be reconstructed from all three Gospels, originally written in Aramaic and changed by each evangelist in his own way;
- by J.G.Herder (1744-1803) in the 'tradition hypothesis': a series of individual traditions of Jesus, handed down orally, which each collected in his own way;
- by F.D.E.Schleiermacher (1768-1834) in the 'fragment' or *diegeseis* hypothesis'; this resembled Herder's solution, but postulated written traditions.

The second model assumes a use of Gospels by others. Here too different variants are possible. The most important are:
- on the one hand the assumption of the priority of Matthew: Mark is a shorter version of Matthew, Luke similarly a model for Mark, himself dependent on or independent of Matthew (Griesbach, Bleek, more recently Farmer);
- on the other hand, Mark as a basis for both Matthew and Luke (thus Lachmann); the extra material in Matthew, above all in the discourses of the 'Sermon on the Mount', thought to be derived from a special Matthaean source; later, along with similar texts in Luke which are independent of Mark, it is thought to be derived from a sayings source common to Matthew and Luke (Weisse), which they had in addition to Mark.

That was the 'two-source theory', which was then confirmed and developed by H.J.Holtzmann in 1863 in his work *Die synoptischen Evangelien*. It is still largely accepted as the solution of the 'synoptic problem'. It contains clear elements of both basic models: along with the second model it assumes the dependence of both Matthew and Luke on Mark; along with the first it takes into account common traditions (oral or written) which have not been preserved as such. The terms used to describe these are 'logia source' (named after a fruitful misunderstanding of an old piece of information that Matthew collected 'Logia of Jesus' in the Hebrew language), or 'sayings source' (Q, short for German *Quelle*).

Theologically, the two-source theory meant that people now thought that they had the reliable sources they were seeking for a historical picture of Jesus: Mark for the chronological course of his life, Q for the content of his preaching. Like John, Matthew and Luke were initially excluded, but they did contain a substantial amount of the preaching of

Jesus, especially the basis of the Sermon on the Mount. At all times this had been as it were the foundation document of Christianity, and as such it was not (completely) lost now.

The two-source theory was renewed and supplemented by B.H. Streeter, who in his book *The Four Gospels* (Macmillan 1924) summed up the results of earlier British scholarship. He postulated further sources for the special material in Matthew and Luke respectively.

The following phenomena need explanation:

– the surplus ('special material') which appears in only one of the Gospels. There is not much in Mark; in Matthew it appears especially in connection with the theme of the law; and in Luke in particular there are long narrative parables (e.g. the 'Prodigal Son', Luke 15.11-32). In the case of Matthew and Luke do these derive from further sources (thus Streeter): S^Matt and S^Luke and/or from the evangelists themselves?

– the agreements between Matthew and Luke against Mark, although there is a theory that each is dependent on Mark and not on Q ('minor agreements', e.g. in Mark 12.28-34 par.): was the Gospel of Mark which Matthew and Luke used another (earlier? later?) version than the one that we know?

– the divergences between Matthew and Luke in texts which in theory belong to Q (e.g. Matt.22.1-14/Luke 14.16-24); was Q in an identical (written? oral?) form in both texts or in differing versions (Q^Matt and Q^Luke) and/or did the evangelists alter these, or was Q composed in Aramaic, coming down to the evangelists in different Greek translations (thus especially J.Wellhausen)?

It should be stressed that the two-source theory is still a theory, though in comparison with other theories it seems to be the one which leaves the least unexplained. However, it cannot completely solve all the questions which arise. For exegetical work on the Gospel texts there are various synopses, i.e. books in which related sections are printed in parallel.

– The structure of the *Synopsis of the First Three Gospels* by A.Huck, most recently edited by H.Lietzmann (Blackwell 1976), is most clearly based on the two-source theory (cf. also the list of parallels on pp.xiii-xx): Mark provides the outline and Q material is included in context in both Matthew and Luke. However, if the order in Matt. and/or Luke differs, the parallel texts appear there only once (there is an English translation: Burton Throckmorton, *Gospel Parallels*, Nelson [4]1979);

– in principle, K.Aland's *Synopsis Quattuor Evangeliorum* (Deutsche Bibelgesellschaft [12]1982, has a similar structure, except that it also includes the whole text of the Gospel of John; the text and text-critical apparatus are identical with N^{26} (see 2.1.5);

– the *Synopsis* by H.Greeven (as a successor to that of Huck, it is simply called 'Huck/Greeven', Eerdmans and Paternoster Press 1981, but in fact it has been completely redone) follows a new course, in that it is not based on the two-source theory but takes more account than others of the connections within the Gospels (cf. especially the juxtaposition of the various announcements of the passion, 32f.). The text and text-critical apparatus are independent; John is used where the content is close to that of the synoptics;

– there is a reconstructed Q text in A.Polag, *Fragmenta Q*, 1979, while S.Schulz, *Griechisch-deutsche Synopse der Q-Überlierungen*, 1972, prints the text in parallel columns;

– among English synopses mention should also be made of that by H.F.D.Sparks, *A Synopsis of the Four Gospels* (two vols.), A.& C.Black 1970, 1974. The first volume prints the English text of the synoptic Gospels with Johannine parallels and the second the text of the Gospel of John with synoptic parallels.

When working with a synopsis it is worth highlighting in different colours what is common to two or more Gospels, in order to bring out what the Gospels have in common and thus also where they differ (use one colour for what is common to all three, one for what is common to Matthew and Luke, one for what is in common to Mark and Matthew and one for what is in common to Mark and Luke); even individual letters can be marked where there are different forms of the same word.

In addition to the 'synoptic problem' proper, the literary-critical question also arises in the case of Mark itself, since there are many indications that it too goes back to already existing sources. It also arises in the case of Q, in so far as the text common to Matthew and Luke can be the final stage of a lengthy development. In the case of John, too, the question arises as to whether the author used sources and, if so, how they relate to the tradition common to the synoptic Gospels. As Paul himself occasionally indicates that he is not using words of his own but quoting, here too literary-critical questions ultimately arise.

2.2.5 Literary criticism as exegetical questioning

The defining question for literary criticism:

What texts which are already in existence does the author work into his text?

The following auxiliary questions help to answer this question:

At what points does the author himself point out that he is taking over a text which has already been formulated (e.g. OT quotations or I Cor.11.23)?

At what points are there breaks or seams in the text (e.g. can Mark 2.5, 10 or II Cor.2.12f.; 7.5 be read one after the other, without the sense that something is missing?)

At what points is part of a text in tension with its context, in a way which cannot be explained as being how the author wanted to shape it (e.g. John 14.31; 18.1 in relation to John 15-17).

Are there parallel texts which are independent of the present text (e.g. the eucharistic tradition in I Cor.11.23-25 in connection with Mark 14.22-24)? Does the terminology of a text differ significantly from the terminology used by an author elsewhere (e.g. Rom.3.25)?

In the case of the synoptic Gospels, if one posits the two-source theory for Matthew and Luke, it follows that these take up either Mark or Q or special material. A comparison between Matthew or Luke and Mark creates criteria which define how much of the working over is by Matthew and how much by Luke; from this, conclusions can be drawn as to how much each has worked over Q, and this also helps to define the involvement of the evangelist in question in the special material.

In the case of Mark literary-critical work is far more difficult. Various explanations which he thinks he must give his readers (e.g. Mark 7.3f.) suggest that he is handing on to them material which is no longer comprehensible as it stands, though it was immediately comprehensible to earlier listeners and readers. That leads to the assumption that Mark will have had traditions which had already been formulated and which he puts in the context of his Gospel. There is, of course, a good deal of uncertainty as to their extent or even wording; above all – and at this point a comment must be made by way of anticipation – extent and wording relate to decisions which are made from the perspective of form criticism (see 3.2) and redaction criticism (see 3.3).

In the case of the Gospel of John the attentive reader will be struck by the double conclusion to the book in 20.30f. and 21.24f.; no one would expect from 20.30f. that another chapter was going to follow. This chapter contains stories of appearances in Galilee (thus also Matt.28.16-20), whereas those in John 20 are located in Jerusalem (thus also Luke 24.13-53). John 21 is an appendix in which the relationship of the 'beloved disciple' to Peter is an issue (21.15-23), and in the second conclusion to the book the whole Gospel is attributed to this disciple.

John 14.31 is directly continued in 18.1, whereas chapters 15 to 17 look like an insertion. In another way that can also be conjectured for 6.(48?,) 51c-58, because here eucharistic terminology interrupts the imagery of the bread of life in a very crude way; or for 6.39b, 40b and other passages, which contain a reference to a future end of the world, in contrast to the theme pervasive elsewhere that the coming of the Son into the world is already judgment on the world.

Thus in literary-critical terms various indications in the Gospel point to at least two overlapping strata. (By contrast, where 7.53-8.11 belongs is a problem for textual criticism rather than literary criticism, see 2.1.5.) We can also see a basic stratum in the miracle stories, some of which are very similar to those in the synoptic Gospels (above all John 6.1-26, with the same connection between feeding and walking on the lake as in Mark 6.32-52, though in the discourse which follows in John only the motif of the bread is then taken up) and those in 2.11 and 4.54 which are numbered as the first and second signs. By contrast, the long discourses which are the special characteristic of the Fourth Gospel have no real parallels in the synoptics. Finally, the passion narrative has a whole series of features in common with the synoptic passion narratives, though there are also considerable differences. Both here and in the case of the miracle stories one can assume either a direct link with the synoptics (all of them?) or the use of common traditions which came to both the synoptics and John by different ways.

In the case of Acts in principle we have to reckon similarly with the incorporation of already formulated tradition, but since it has been worked over in a uniform way by Luke it is more difficult to identify, especially as Luke does not indicate anywhere in the text that he is quoting from sources. The striking transition from the third-person narrative to the first-person plural with the use of 'we' in 20.5-15; 21.1-18; 27.1-16 (and in the manuscript D in 11.28) seems to indicate a source produced by someone involved, but it is better explained as a stylistic means used by the narrator. Nor do the differences in the three accounts of Paul's conversion (9.1-19; 22.3-21; 26.9-20) indicate different sources; they differ because of the different positions of the speeches in the structure of the work. We may assume that a list of stages ('itinerary') is used for Paul's journeys from 13.1 (the clearest literary-critical indication would be the twofold mention of Derbe in 14.6,20b), but here too we cannot define its extent.

In the case of argumentative texts the literary-critical question is quite different from that in the narrative texts, since here the author is not primarily handing on tradition which has come down to him, but formulating the text himself throughout. Nevertheless there is a series of passages in the letters of Paul in which he himself indicates that he is quoting. First, of course, come scriptural quotations (here the Greek translation, and not the Hebrew text, is presupposed), including a text in I Cor.2.9 which is identified as a quotation but which does not occur in that form in the Old Testament (cf. also Eph.5.14). However, a quotation from the Greek author Menander in I Cor.15.33 is not identified as such (but see the quotation in Titus 1.12; Epimenides is meant).

Secondly, in I Cor.11.23 and 15.3 Paul indicates that he has handed on to his readers what he himself received; the terms *paralambanein* and *paradidonai* used here are terms from the communication of tradition: the Hebrew equivalents are *qbl* (see Kabbala) and *msr* (see Masora). Thus Paul is indicating that the texts which follow already had a particular wording which he has adopted: in the case of the eucharistic tradition in I Cor.15.3-5 the parallel construction of the sentences points to this, as do words which are not customary in Paul (Paul then expands the tradition from 15.6 on). But presumably other passages like e.g. Rom.1.3f.; 3.26, which differ from the context in terminology and content, also go back to already existing tradition, though Paul does not describe them as quotations but takes them up completely into his own train of argument. The same is also true of Phil.2.6-11, a hymn to Christ in two strophes (there are further such hymns in Col.1.15-20; I Tim.3.16).

The tradition also includes sayings of Jesus which are described as such, though Paul takes these up only very rarely: I Thess.4.15; I Cor.7.10; 9.13. In all passages they are treated differently from the Old Testament texts, but they are not really quotations, since in I Thess.4.15 the 'we' is unthinkable in a saying of Jesus, and the two passages in I Corinthians only quote sayings of Jesus indirectly.

Finally, we must recognize that at least II Corinthians is not a single letter which Paul wrote in this form from first sentence to last, but a collection of parts of his letters made by a later hand. This is indicated by the different situation in 10-13 (a row with the community) from that in 1-9 (reconciliation with the community), the duplication of chapters 8 and 9 about the collection, and finally the seams at 2.12f. and 7.6. By contrast the section 6.14-7.1 is theologically so different from what we know of Paul elsewhere that there is much to be said for assuming that here we have the insertion of a text which is not Paul's (the proximity to the theology of the Qumran texts is particularly striking here). It has been conjectured that other letters of Paul, too, are compilations by a later hand, as in the case of II Corinthians. But at all events that can still be explained in the case of Philippians by Paul being in different situations in 1.1-3.1 (where he is in prison) and 3.2-4.3 (where he is free); 4.10-20 would then have been added to these two parts of the letter as a thanksgiving for a gift from the Philippians.

In the Catholic Letters the best literary-critical explanation of the relationship between Jude and II Peter would seem to be that Jude was the model for II Peter. The conclusion to I John in 5.13 is striking; it is followed by a further summary entreaty: from a literary-critical perspective this is perhaps an indication of later revision, though it could also be explained in stylistic terms.

In the Revelation of John the different hymn passages (4.11, etc.) were perhaps taken over by the author from the worship of his community.

In the defining question and the references to literary-critical questioning which follow, the approach has been deliberately neutralized in that it is now no longer formulated as a question of theological truth, as it originally was in the historical theology of the nineteenth century. The reason for this is that this question of truth can no longer be put simply as a historical question, as will emerge from the further exegetical questioning which follows. At the same time this relativizes literary criticism, since other disciplines take further the discussion of many phenomena in the text which scholars think should be explained in literary-critical terms or which were hardly considered when literary criticism was so predominant.

2.3   The question of the setting of the New Testament in the world of its time: the history of religions

2.3.1   The basic problem

The basic problem of the history of religions as a set of exegetical questions lies in the insight that early Christianity is not fully and in any point different from contemporary religions. Rather, there are many connections both with contemporary Judaism and with the Hellenistic religions of the time, but Christianity here cannot be said in principle to be prior in either content or time. Whereas the history of religions is concerned with religions generally, history-of-religions questions within New Testament exegesis are concerned with the relationship between early Christianity and contemporary historical phenomena.

2.3.2   Points to which the New Testament relates

Relations to the Old Testament, which can be seen simply from the way in which it is quoted in the New, were unproblematical as long as the Bible was understood as a unity or this unity could be seen in terms of a progressive development from Old Testament to New – regardless of how that was defined more closely. References to Judaism after the Old Testament (this Wellhausen referred to with the term 'late' Judaism, which has negative connotations) had been noted since Christian theologians began to occupy themselves with Jewish tradition, above all in the Talmud. The Talmud (see 2.3.3) was printed for the first time in Venice in 1519-1523. J.Reuchlin (1455-1522) used this tradition, which he studied with Jewish teachers, to interpret the Bible. The writings of Philo of Alexandria and Josephus (see 2.3.4) had been handed down in the Christian tradition; both authors almost had the status of church fathers.

However, after humanism a concern with the classical Greek tradition in the original language had also come into the foreground for theology – from the Reformation onwards, knowledge of Greek was a prerequisite for the study of theology. A summary of such work on the New Testament is represented by the *Novum Testamentum Graecum* of Johann Jakob Wettstein (1693-1754), which was published in 1751/52: a text-critical apparatus was followed by a second apparatus with information about parallels in Jewish and Greek tradition. In the nineteenth century, knowledge of what was originally both Jewish and Greek literature developed considerably, to the same degree and conditioned by the same factors as study of the manuscripts of the New Testament (see 2.1.4). Searches of the libraries of the East and even at that time archaeological discoveries produced not only Greek texts but above all writings of Jewish origin which enjoyed canonical respect in Eastern churches (Syria, Ethiopia); although originally written in Hebrew or Aramaic, they were now extant only in translations.

This considerably shifted the framework of reference for the interpretation of the New Testament, though to begin with systematic use was not made of the new material. Some material discovered in this way became available to an English-speaking readership in R.H.Charles, *The Apocrypha and Pseudepigrapha of the Old Testament*, published by Oxford University Press in 1913, which provided a modern translation; this had been preceded by a similar volume in Germany, edited by E.Kautzsch.

The first volume edited by Charles contains the Apocrypha of the Old Testament, i.e. those writings which are in the Septuagint but not in the Hebrew Bible and therefore were not taken into Protestant Bibles; the second volume, *Pseudepigrapha* (the term was defined as those writings which are falsely attributed to some prominent figure from Hebrew antiquity), contains writings above all from apocalyptic, e.g. the Book of Enoch which was handed down in Ethiopic or the Book of Baruch which was handed down in Syriac, but also IV Ezra (a work which in the Vulgate is part of the Old Testament).

The significance of such writings for the interpretation of the New Testament became clear in Johannes Weiss's book *Jesus' Proclamation of the Kingdom of God* (1892, English translation Fortress Press and SCM Press 1971), in which he worked out that 'kingdom of God' had a future meaning, even for Jesus himself. This contrasted with the interpretation of 'kingdom of God' predominant in the nineteenth century, as an ideal within this world to be striven for through culture, education and work. Now alien elements in Jesus and in early Christianity came to the fore, even more in Albert Schweitzer's portrait of Jesus as a failed apocalyptist (see 2.4.2.4). In his book *Die Religion des Judentums im späthellenistischen Zeitalter* (The Religion of Judaism in the late-Hellenistic Period, 1902; [3]1926, edited by H.Gressmann), Wilhelm Bousset gave a systematic summary account of a new picture of Judaism at the time of early Christianity which had been obtained in this way.

Another branch of study, which began primarily from ancient philology (represented by A.Dietrich and R.Reitzenstein), was the investigation of 'Gnosticism'. The nineteenth-century editions of the church fathers had reminded scholars of the controversies of the fathers with the so-called 'Gnostics'; however, the latter were seen predominantly through the eyes of the church fathers as those who had falsified Christian doctrine and speculated in remarkable systems which were inevitably not very attractive to historical-critical theology. New texts including the *Corpus Hermeticum* (after the Greek God Hermes, who is evidently also the Egyptian God Thoth), which was handed down through the Middle Ages, Greek texts (magical papyri, the 'Mithras liturgy'), and not least texts from Iranian (Nietzsche's Zarathustra) and Indian religions which had a very great influence in their time now made it seem conceivable that the 'Gnostics' were in no way to be understood merely as a group on the periphery of early Christianity, but rather that they were a Christian variant of a comprehensive world religion, 'Gnosticism', which existed before and alongside Christianity, and that they shared this character with the whole of the early Christian community in the Hellenistic sphere and large parts of Judaism.

The basic structure was seen to be a myth which explains the existing world from the evil will of a creator (demiurge) who is distinct from the good God and/or from the fall of good matter into chaos, i.e. into the existing world. Redemption means the return of this good matter from chaos to its own home, the good light world above, and this takes place through the descent of the redeemer, who gathers together the sparks of light that have been dispersed in chaos and brings them above. It is clear that the christology of the Gospel of John or Paul appears as a variant of the redeemer myth if it is seen against the background of this model and if the model is assumed to be pre-Christian. Thus Reitzenstein arrived at the maxim 'Paul is a Gnostic' and Bultmann at his definition 'Primitive Christianity as a syncretistic phenomenon' (i.e. as a religion which has been influenced in various ways by both Judaism and Hellenism).

R.Reitzenstein, *Die hellenistischen Mysterienreligionen*, [3]1927, 348;

R.Bultmann, *Primitive Christianity in its Earliest Setting*, Thames and Hudson 1956, title to Chapter V.1.

For texts see Bentley Layton, *The Gnostic Scriptures*, Doubleday and SCM Press 1987.

See also K.Rudolph, *Gnosis. The Nature and History of an Ancient Religion*, T.& T.Clark 1983.

   This is also the context of the Mandaean texts which became known in the course of the 1920s; the Mandaeans are a group which still exists in Iraq and has a special understanding of baptism; John the Baptist is very important for them. These texts were utilized especially by W.Bauer and R.Bultmann in their commentaries on the Gospel of John.

For the Mandaeans see E.S.Drower, *The Mandaeans of Iraq and Iran. Their Cults, Customs, Magic, Legends and Folklore*, Oxford University Press 1937 (Lady Drower also edited Mandaean texts, published by E.J.Brill, Leiden)

Rudolf Bultmann, *The Gospel of John*, Blackwell and Westminster Press 1971.

Finally, new light was also shed on the Greek used by the New Testament writers. Previously it had been seen largely as a special language in comparison with the literary tradition of ancient philosophers, historians and poets, but as a result of studies of the newly discovered papyri, which were made especially by A.Deissmann, a different picture emerged. Here in bills, lists and letters, but also in religious texts, it was possible to.discover everyday language as it was spoken and written at the time of early Christianity, so-called *koine*. And it proved that the Greek of the New Testament authors was not a special language, still less a sacred language, but corresponded to everyday language (the exception was the Letter to the Hebrews with its attractive Greek).

A.Deissmann, *Light from the Ancient East*, Hodder and Stoughton [2]1927.

This material was systematically evaluated in E.Preuschen, *Wörterbuch zum Neuen Testament*, which W.Bauer (see I.2.4) then later revised fully (see the information about sources in the bibliography).

2.3.3   The history-of-religions school

All in all, in this way the picture that scholars had had of early Christianity and its texts shifted very considerably. Its primary framework of interpretation was no longer the Old Testament and the classical Greek tradition but new and hitherto largely unknown texts, which could only seem late when measured by the criterion of the classics or the Old Testament (from 'late Judaism' and 'late antiquity'). But above all early Christianity inevitably seemed strange by comparison with the Protestant church and theology at the turn of the century.

And if historical theology had sought to safeguard that which was historically unique and underivable as the starting point of Christianity by using literary criticism to define what historical sources were reliable, now the 'history of religions school' relativized early Christianity, making it a particular instance of the general religious feeling of the Hellenistic period.

Initially the nucleus of the 'history-of-religions school' was a group of young scholars who had got to know one another in Göttingen: A.Eichhorn, W.Bousset, J.Weiss, W.Wrede and P.Wernle; later they were joined by W.Heitmüller and P.Gressmann. They engaged in constant discussion and championed a joint programme, which even extended to church politics. By means of individual studies (Religions-geschichtliche Volksbücher) and a commentary series on the New Testament (Die Schriften des Neuen Testaments) they attempted to make their views known to a wider public. Their work was systematically taken up by E.Troeltsch (see 2.4.2), above all in his works *The Absoluteness of Christianity* (1902) and 'On historical and dogmatic method in theology' (1898) (see 2.4.2.2).

As a countermove to this, an attempt was made to understand both the language and content of the New Testament not from Hellenism but above all from the Old Testament, with (late) Judaism as an intermediary. Here mention should be made of the dogmatic and above all the exegetical works of Adolf Schlatter (1852-1938 – he wrote commentaries on the whole of the New Testament). But above all mention should be made of the monumental work by Paul Billerbeck (the Old Testament scholar H.L.Strack, who was more famous in his time, lent his name to the work simply in order to make publication possible).

Kommentar zum Neuen Testament aus Talmud und Midrasch, which appeared in four volumes between 1922 and 1928 (there are two index volumes edited by J.Jeremias, which appeared in 1956 and 1961).

Here, in the order of the New Testament writings, comparative material is given from texts of the Jewish tradition; the fourth volume (in two parts) contains systematic excursuses on specific themes.

As the title shows, Billerbeck relied predominantly on the Jewish tradition as it had been collected after the destruction of Jerusalem by the Romans in 70 CE. This happened first in the Talmud (from *lmd* = learn). Its basis is the Mishnah (from the Hebrew *snh* = repeat), a collection of oral tradition alongside the 'Old' Testament, the extent of which was also fixed at this time. It consists of 63 (originally 60) tractates, which are brought together in six groups. They are quoted by tractate, chapter, individual saying (e.g. Sanh[edrin] 10,4). Sayings (all different) by scribes on specific issues are listed. The collection was closed towards the end of the second century. Its aim was to secure the tradition which had been endangered by the catastrophe (e.g. rules for sacrifice for the time when a new temple was built).

The Mishnah was developed into the Talmud in two versions, the Palestinian or Jerusalem Talmud and the Babylonian Talmud. To the Mishnah was added the Gemara (from Hebrew *gmr*, expand), further traditions on individual sections of the Mishnah. However, the Palestinian Talmud has such Gemara only on thirty-nine tractates and the Babylonian Talmud (though it is much larger) on thirty six and a half. The Talmud is quoted by tractate, page number in the printed editions, recto (a) or verso (b) (e.g. bSanh 89a). One can tell whether the quotation is from the Palestinian or the Jerusalem Talmud by a prefixed p or j (pSanh or jSanh), but these prefixes are often left out, as the Babylonian Talmud is cited so much more often.

Commentaries on biblical writings are called Midrash (plural Midrashim; from Hebrew *drs*, search).

Introduction and texts
R.C.Musaph Andriesse, *From Torah to Kabbalah*, SCM Press and Oxford University Press, New York 1981, provides a basic introduction.
For the Mishnah, the standard edition is R.C.Danby, *The Mishnah*, Oxford University Press 1933.
For the Babylonian Talmud, see the Soncino Talmud, published between 1935 and 1952 under the editorship of I.Epstein.

Finally, the *Theological Dictionary of the New Testament* (*TDNT*) belongs in this context – or at least its first volumes do. This was edited from 1933 by Gerhard Kittel and then after 1945 brought to completion by G.Friedrich. An English translation was begun in 1964 and completed soon after the last volume of the German appeared in 1979. In 1928 Kittel had planned an extent of two volumes which were to appear within three years. The work began as a continuation of the Lexicon by H.Cremer, which was at the opposite pole to Deissmann (see

G.Friedrich, 'Prehistory of the Theological Dictionary of the New Testament', *TDNT* 10, 613-61); a typical feature of the early volumes of *TDNT* is that for the most part they dispute that the 'concepts' of the New Testament have any connection with Hellenism – the words may be Greek, but the content comes only from the Old Testament. In addition, in many articles an attempt is made to derive the 'real' meaning of a word from its etymology.

After the Second World War there were two further great discoveries of texts: the Qumran scrolls, written predominantly in Hebrew, and the thirteen codexes in Coptic (or late Egyptian) from Nag Hammadi in Upper Egypt; as a result of these two finds both Judaism and Gnosticism proved to be much more differentiated than had been thought.

The Qumran texts contained manuscripts of the Bible which were important for the textual criticism of the Old Testament, but in particular the group's own texts. They had left this library when their settlement was destroyed by the Romans; it also contains texts which cannot be directly attributed to them but which are also in their library.

This group was probably Essene. The Essenes are known to us from ancient literature but remarkably, unlike the Pharisees and Sadducees, they are not mentioned in the New Testament. The reason for their separation from the Jerusalem temple was their own interpretation of the law, in which e.g. a calendar orientated on the solar year had an important role. With its help it was possible to avoid conflicts between what the law laid down about the arrangements necessary for feast days and the rules for observing the sabbath, because in this calendar none of the high festivals would fall on a sabbath.

Geza Vermes, *The Dead Sea Scrolls in English*, Penguin Books [3]1987.
For the significance of the texts see Geza Vermes, *The Dead Sea Scrolls. Qumran in Perspective*, SCM Press and Fortress Press [2]1982;
Michael A.Knibb, *The Qumran Community*, Cambridge University Press 1987.

These texts are cited with a Q and a prefixed number, which shows in which of the caves (there are eleven in all) the particular writing was found; this is followed by an abbreviation which stands for the relevant scroll (initially abbreviations of a title were used, but then usually consecutive numbers).

The codexes from Nag-Hammadi contain primarily (though not exclusively) texts from the sphere of Gnosticism, which hitherto had been known only from polemical reports by 'orthodox' church fathers. They show that Gnosticism is more differentiated internally than these reports suggest, and is more than just a system. The best known of these texts is the Gospel of Thomas, a sequence of sayings of Jesus and very occasionally brief scenes; on the whole it recalls texts of the canonical

Gospels which are familiar to us, but there are differences from them which confuse the reader. There is controversy as to whether the Gospel of Thomas presupposes the canonical Gospels and is a development from them (this is the predominant view in Germany) or is a separate branch of the Jesus tradition.

For translations in English:
The Nag Hammadi Library, ed. J.M.Robinson, E.J.Brill ²1984;
Bentley Layton, *The Gnostic Scriptures*, Doubleday and SCM Press 1987.
The Gospel of Thomas is printed in Latin, English and German translations in Appendix I to the synopsis by K.Aland.

All in all, at present a degree of balance has been achieved in that Judaism and Hellenism are not understood as being in strict opposition; Judaism in the Hellenistic period is seen rather as part of Hellenism and as the distinctive framework of interpretation for at least the first and second generations of early Christianity. The Greek tradition will also have been communicated through it. From the wealth of literature mention should be made of:

E.Lohse, *The New Testament Environment*, Abingdon Press and SCM Press 1976;
Calvin J.Roetzel, *The World that Shaped the New Testament*, John Knox Press and SCM Press 1987;
Helmut Koester, *Introduction to the New Testament*, I. *History, Culture and Religion of the Hellenistic Age*; II. *History and Literature of Early Christianity*, De Gruyter 1982;
C.K.Barrett, *The New Testament Background: Selected Documents*, SPCK ²1987;
M.Rostovtzeff, *The Social and Economic History of the Roman Empire*, Oxford University Press 1926;
id., *The Social and Economic History of the Hellenistic World*, Oxford University Press 1941 (three vols.);
M.Hengel, *Judaism and Hellenism*, SCM Press and Fortress Press 1974;
E.Schürer, *A History of the Jewish People in the Age of Jesus Christ* I-III (revised edition by G.Vermes, F.Millar and M.Black), T.& T.Clark 1973-88;
E.M.Meyers and J.F.Strange, *Archaeology, the Rabbis and Early Christianity*, Abingdon Press and SCM Press 1981;
A.R.C.Leaney, *The Jewish and Christian World. 200 BC to AD 200*, Cambridge University Press 1988.

2.3.4   The history of religions as exegetical questioning

The defining question for the history of religions is:
    In what context of questions of their time are the statements in New Testament texts to be put?

The auxiliary questions are:

Are there parallels in content to individual statements or themes of the text in the New Testament itself, in Judaism, in the Old Testament or in Greek texts?

What keywords or themes from problems of the time are taken up? Does this allow us to argue to a tradition which has been formed? Are only partial elements of a fixed tradition recognizable?

In the case of Old Testament quotations: which form of the text is cited? How was the text cited understood in Judaism or early Christianity?

How does the author relate to traditional views?

Here too the defining question is again much more formal than the original approach, again above all because the question of 'truth' is bracketed off, since it is not seen simply in an overarching Hellenistic religious sense or in a connection between the tradition and the Old Testament and Judaism. Rather, history-of-religions investigations are meant primarily to help to clarify the difference between the presuppositions and associations of the readers of the time and ours today. Both socially and culturally, we live in a very different world from the world of that time, so historical knowledge is needed to explain New Testament texts.

However, our present associations are also influenced by our familiarity with biblical texts and with the Christian tradition generally, and by the way in which translations are related to our present-day speech. In all this various traditions overlap, sometimes with considerable differences in understanding. The aim of work in the history of religions is to prevent the texts being dominated by our present associations.

The term 'tradition history' is often used instead of 'history of religions', especially for connections between the New Testament and the Old Testament and Judaism. But in addition, tradition history is also used to denote the history of the transmission of the tradition – e.g. from Jesus to the Gospels.

The framework of reference for understanding the synoptic Gospels is Judaism at the time of Jesus and early Christianity. At each stage of the interpretation, but also simply when we are retelling these texts, we need information: e.g. about Pharisees, high priests, Pilate, etc.; about habits and customs, norms and rules of behaviour, questions and solutions discussed at this time in this context. On occasion, the evangelists themselves have already inserted such information (e.g. Mark 7.31f.), because they evidently thought that their readers no longer had any direct access to it.

The fact that the Jesus tradition is in Greek, whereas Jesus himself spoke Aramaic, also indicates a change of tradition to another cultural sphere. However, the information which the Gospels give us about Judaism is very crude when judged by the picture that we can construct from history: this crudeness can be seen in the way in which 'the Pharisees' are seen as a closed group, in purely negative terms, or in the ideas which the evangelists seem to have about the geography of Palestine. If we want to understand Jesus, we must try to clarify the questions which he took up and also the significance e.g. of 'kingdom of God' at that time as a future entity, or of 'Son of man' not as a complement to 'Son of God' in the context of the doctrine of the two natures ('true man and true God'), but as a judge expected at the end. The whole of the tradition which begins with Jesus and has its final form in the Gospels is also connected with the history of Judaism; thus in Mark we can see the situation of the Jewish War (Mark 13) and in Matthew the controversy with rabbinic Judaism, the form of Judaism which arose after the Jewish War.

Our most important source for contemporary Jewish history is the Jewish writer Josephus (he was born in 37/38 CE and died at the beginning of the second century). He himself played a leading role in the 'Jewish War' of 66-70 CE and later described this war from the Roman perspective; he described the Jewish tradition in his *Jewish Antiquities* and defended it against pagan attacks in his book *Against Apion*.

See T.Rajak, *Josephus*, Duckworth and Fortress Press 1983.
There is an English translation of the *Jewish War*, Penguin Books [2]1981. Parallel Greek and English texts of this, *Against Apion*, and the *Jewish Antiquities* are published in the Loeb Classical Library.

The 'history-of-religions problem' is more closely bound up with the interpretation of the Gospel of John than with that of any other New Testament writing. The problem arises from the way in which Jesus speaks so differently in it from his manner in the synoptic Gospels – in long discourses the themes of which are hard to separate. Jesus speaks above all of himself as the Son sent from heaven who returns to his Father, and who in the 'I am' sayings presents himself as the fulfilment of elemental human hopes for bread, life, truth, etc. In addition, throughout the Gospel there is opposition ('dualism') between above and below, light and darkness, truth and life, etc. as mutually exclusive definitions of the origin of Jesus and the believers on the one hand, and the world on the other.

Here we find a particularly abrupt contrast between an interpretation within the framework of Gnosticism (which we find above all in Bultmann's commentary) and one within the framework of Judaism (not least as experienced through the Qumran texts).

What is true of the Gospel of John is also true of the letters of Paul. Even if Paul was a Jew by birth and upbringing (cf. above all Phil.3.5f.), he came from the Diaspora and worked as a Christian missionary in a Greek-speaking environment. His Bible was not the Hebrew Bible, but the Greek Old Testament, as the quotations make clear. The Christianity which he represents and which he helped to create in the communities that he founded is not in direct continuity with the original circle of Jesus' disciples, but existed from the beginning in the conditions of the great Hellenistic cities with its own new questions, forms of organization and developing norms of conduct.

Since the historical theology of the nineteenth century was orientated above all on a portrait of the historical Jesus, Paul was put in the shade as being a 'dogmatic theologian'. A historical view which goes back to the history-of-religions school is still influential today, namely that Jesus and Paul cannot be directly compared, but are separated first by the primitive Palestinian community which spoke Aramaic and then by the Hellenistic community which spoke Greek. With all kinds of modifications, this picture of history still influences not only books about the history of earliest Christianity but also introductions and theologies.

It has replaced the picture developed by F.C.Baur (see 2.4.1), who saw the mainstream church ('early Catholicism', or whatever it is called) as developing gradually out of the antithesis of Jewish Christianity and Gentile Christianity. This antithesis is now no longer seen as a systematic opposition but rather as a historical development, but above all the transition to Hellenism is thought already to take place in earliest Christianity itself, rather than being alienation or apostasy from primitive Christianity in the second century.

The easiest way to be clear about the phenomenon as such is to see how Billerbeck (2.3.3) offers significantly less help for interpreting the Gospel of John or Paul than in the area of the synoptic Gospels. However, the change in our image of Judaism and of Gnosticism has also had an effect on the interpretation of Paul, so that for example the interpretation of Rom.5.12ff. (Adam and Christ) is no longer limited to the alternative whether Paul is working with the Gnostic redeemer myth or only with Genesis 1f.; the associations prove to be much more complex if one goes through the various Jewish interpretations of Gen. 1f.

The same is true of the interpretation of the various christological titles (Lord, Son of God, Christ, Redeemer, etc). Nineteenth-century historical theology saw these as an alien understanding of Jesus, because they dogmatized his human form (see 2.4.2.3); this was partly endorsed by the fact that they were derived from Hellenism, and to this degree the history-of-religions school remained within the framework of this historical theology. But here too the connections again seem more complex.

At all events, for the interpretation of Paul, including the question of the opponents whom Paul has to combat in his letters, we need not only a knowledge of Judaism but also a knowledge of the history of the Hellenistic period in the broadest sense (the history of its spirituality, religion, culture, society, etc.) – that period whose legacy was increasingly taken over by the Roman empire.

The Acts of the Apostles is the closest of all New Testament writings to the Hellenistic world because of the way in which its form links it to ancient historiography. Indeed its aim is to describe how Christianity came via Greece to the centre of the empire. It is written from the standpoint of someone living one or two generations after these beginnings, when Christianity was already understanding itself as an established movement in this world, and one which had a future.

In the way in which it deals with the Old Testament, the Letter to the Hebrews proves to be very close to the interpretation of scripture that we find in Philo of Alexandria. The only date we can connect with Philo is 40 CE, when he was part of a delegation of Jews from Alexandria to Rome; among his works, the tradition of which is generally good, are a commentary on Genesis and a systematic description of the 'legislation of Moses'.

Greek and English texts of Philo's works are published in the Loeb Classical Library. For Genesis see Vol.1 and for the Decalogue see Vol.7.

Finally, the significance of the history-of-religions approach to the Revelation of John was shown by Hermann Gunkel in his book *Schöpfung und Chaos in Urzeit und Endzeit* (Creation and Chaos in Primal Time and End Time) which appeared in 1895. In contrast to the interpretation of Revelation in terms of contemporary events, which had been customary previously, Gunkel pointed out how much not only individual images but also whole complexes of motifs were governed by ancient traditions.

2.4   Results and open questions of historical theology

2.4.1   Results

It has emerged from the above account of the individual complexes of exegetical questions which still tend to be raised today how widely the questions, possible solutions and indeed aporias of contemporary exegesis are governed by the historical criticism of the end of the nineteenth and beginning of the twentieth centuries.

To sum up, let me repeat these once more:

– Textual criticism: present-day textual criticism is inconceivable without the manuscript discoveries, criteria for classifying and evaluating manuscripts, and above all editions of texts from the nineteenth century, even if details of the picture have shifted;

– Literary criticism: the basic possibilities for solving the synoptic problem were worked out in the nineteenth century, especially the two-source theory; more recent attempts in this sphere only modify older proposals for a solution;

– The history of religions: the connections between early Christianity and the Judaism of its time and the way in which it is embedded in the Hellenistic world, along with collections of texts which came into being at that time, still provide points of reference for the interpretation of New Testament texts; the picture of the history of early Christianity which was developed in the history-of-religions school is still a determining factor today.

All this relates to the foundations of research, and it is astonishing what was done by far fewer New Testament scholars than there are in our day, with much more primitive technical means than those at our disposal.

However, the foundations of research also include verdicts on the authenticity and inauthenticity of New Testament writings and the dates to be assigned to them which were essentially developed in the nineteenth century. Here too the framework within which we now move was marked out at that time. This is all the more amazing since these judgments seem to be influenced by a particular picture of history, above all that in Ferdinand Christian Baur (1792-1860), who sought to explain the development of early Christianity from a contrast between Jewish Christianity (represented by Peter and James) and Gentile Christianity (represented by Paul). The assumption that a reduction of this opposition led to the mainstream church of the beginning of the second century made it possible to put individual writings in a chronological order, related to how the degree of opposition to be found in individual instances. So Baur (like others even before him) does not believe that the Pastoral Letters were written by Paul or I Peter by Peter, but in the end regards only four letters (Romans, I Corinthians, II Corinthians and Galatians) as Pauline.

The science of introduction for which Baur laid the foundations is concerned with these questions about the authors of individual writings and their historical context and the audiences whom the author addresses (see 1.3.5). Here, too, the possible solutions discussed in the nineteenth century still have an influence today.

2.4.2   Positions in historical theology

That despite all this we no longer do exegesis as historical criticism is a result of the new theological approach which has come into being since the 1920s and has also influenced exegesis. However, before describing that (see 3.1), I would like to survey four theological positions from the beginning of historical theology which seem to me still to be influential today and which also show the weaknesses and strengths of a theology which takes its credentials from historical criticism: those of Harnack, Troeltsch, Wrede and Schweitzer.

2.4.2.1   Harnack

In the winter semester of 1899/1900 Adolf Harnack (1851-1930; after 1914 he became Adolf von Harnack) gave a series of lectures to an audience from all faculties under the title 'The Essence of Christianity'. They appeared that same year as a book which retained the original character of the lectures. By 1927 it had been reprinted fourteen times and it was translated into fourteen languages.

The title of the English translation is *What is Christianity?*; it was first published in 1900 and reissued with an introduction by Rudolf Bultmann, Harper and Row 1957.

Precisely because of its great popularity, this book can be regarded as typical of a theology which legitimates itself by history and takes only marginal notice of the history-of-religions interpretation which was then beginning.

The book consists of two parts of roughly the same extent: the first is entitled 'The Gospel' and the second 'The Gospel in History'. Under the title 'The Gospel' the preaching of Jesus is described in three sections. The first is concerned with 'The kingdom of God and its coming'. Here Harnack indeed brings in the future interpretation of 'kingdom of God' (see 2.3.3), but subordinates it to what he regards as the real message: 'The kingdom of God comes by coming to the individual, by entering into his soul and laying hold of it' (56). The second section is 'God the Father and the infinite value of the human soul', and the section ends: 'A man may know it or not, but a real reverence for humanity follows fom the practical recognition of God as the Father of us all' (70). Finally, the third section relates to ethics: 'The higher righteousness and the commandment of love'. This is dispositional ethics, and 'the love of one's neighbour is the only practical proof on earth of that love of God which is strong in humility' (52).

So the essence of Christianity is the gospel, and the gospel is none other than the preaching of Jesus as disclosed by historical criticism. Timeless elements are seen as its nucleus, and these have to be extracted from the shell. While Harnack does not dispute that Jesus had a messianic self-awareness or that he was conscious of being Son of God, the messiahship of Jesus does not form the gospel; rather, 'The Gospel, as Jesus proclaimed it, has to do with the Father only and not with the Son' (144). In this way the classical doctrine of the Trinity is transcended, and Jesus' significance is as follows: 'It is not as a mere factor that he is connected with the Gospel; he was its personal realization and its strength, and this he is felt to be still' (145).

Given this definition of the 'essence of Christianity', Harnack now succeeds in taking a stance on such topical problems as the social question, the question of public order and the question of culture, always by reconstructing the preaching of Jesus. Albert Schweitzer bitingly accused him of 'starting out with a gospel which carries him down without difficulty to the year 1899' (*The Quest of the Historical Jesus*, 252, see 2.4.2.4). However, that judgment is already based on the new picture of Jesus with all its alien features. What Harnack wanted to achieve (and indeed was able to achieve) was a 'modern' undogmatic account of Christianity in terms of the present which legitimated itself from a Jesus who is superior to all other attempts, but at the same time is also critical from a liberal Protestant standpoint of other trends of the time, like Socialism. In the second part of the book which, because it is about church history, is of less interest here, this liberal German Protestantism is then described as something which in principle comes very close to a realization of the essence of Christianity.

We read this book nowadays with considerable shaking of the head, taught by more than just the developments in the history of theology which have come about in the meantime. Nevertheless questions need to be remembered for theology and the church:
- How is the 'essence of Christianity' to be defined in view of the context in which church and theology stand, within what we would now call society?
- How is this 'essence' to be shown to be that of Christianity, in view of the historical relativization of any pre-existing metaphysic which has been brought about since historicism?

2.4.2.2   Troeltsch

Ernst Troeltsch (1865-1923) was Professor of Theology in Heidelberg and from 1914 Professor of Philosophy in Berlin; his 'On Historical and Dogmatic Method in Theology' appeared as an article in 1898 in the Studies of the Rhineland Preachers' Association.

Despite its importance, regrettably it has never been translated into English. The original is accessible either in Troeltsch's *Gesammelte Schriften* or reprinted in G.Sauter (ed.), *Theologie als Wissenschaft*, 105-27 (to which page references are given below). Otherwise the reader will have to consult his *The Absoluteness of Christianity*, John Knox Press and SCM Press 1972, the subject-matter of which is related.

Troeltsch begins from the historical method as such, as it had been developed in the sciences during the nineteenth century: 'like modern natural science, a complete revolution in our way of thinking' (110). Its consequences for theology are that: 'The historical method, once applied to biblical scholarship and church history, is a leaven which changes everything and finally bursts out of the whole previous form of theological methods' (106). Its three principles (criticism, analogy and correlation) question all 'purely dogmatic postulates' (107).
- historical criticism can only formulate judgments with degrees of probability (107),
- it can only start fom the basis of the 'similarity in principle of all historical events' (108),
- it can explain these historical events only from the 'interaction of all phenomena of spiritual and historical life' (108).
  Now that means that
- absolute judgments are no longer possible;
- Christianity is no longer to be founded on postulates which cannot be derived from history, but can only be considered in analogy to other developments;
- and historically at any rate, Christianity is to be seen as the 'terminus of antiquity, towards which the great developments of the Near Eastern and the Western world are working and in which very different lines of development finally converge' (109).
  'Anyone who has given it his little finger must also give it whole hand. Therefore from an authentically orthodox standpoint it has a kind of similarity with the devil' (110). Troeltsch sees the consequence of this historical method as being a history-of-religions theology which applies the three principles mentioned above consistently and which is to take the place of the 'dogmatic' method. Quoting himself, he describes as its 'simple result' that 'All human religion is rooted in religious intuition

or divine revelation, which gains the power to share communities from specifically religious personalities and is experienced again by believers with little originality. The belief in God contained in this intuition and concealed in natural religion at the initial stages of a consciousness bound by naturalism finally breaks through this limitation, along with a number of parallel developments in Yahwistic religion and in the proclamation of Jesus which arise out of it, from here on to experience an infinitely rich development. It cannot be calculated in advance, but is always about the life in faith in the living God and the interpretation of any given reality in terms of this faith' (114f.).

By contrast, Troeltsch sees the 'dogmatic method' as being characterized by 'authority': 'It is removed from the overall context of history, analogy with other events and thus from the historical criticism that draws everything into itself and from the uncertainty of its results' (115), and postulates extraordinary saving facts which are elevated above history. In passing, Troeltsch wonders (119) whether one could see the difference between dogmatic and historical method as being identical with the difference between Catholicism and Protestantism, but he rejects this and derives the historical method from the Enlightenment, not from the tradition of the Reformation.

What Troeltsch writes is supported by the 'indispensable presupposition' of belief 'in a reason which rules in history and reveals itself progressively' (121), 'that history is not chaos but presses from unified forces towards a single goal' (122). Certainly 'belief in God in all its forms is in nucleus identical', but it remains limited by the original bond between the human spirit and nature. 'Only at one point has it broken through this limitation, but that is a point which lies at the centre of great religious developments which surround us and come to meet us, in the religion of the prophets of Israel and in the person of Jesus, where the God who is different from nature produces the personality who is superior to nature with its eternally transcendent aims and its force of will that works against the world' (123).

Certainly, then, Troeltsch formulates a definition of the essence of Christianity which is very similar to that of Harnack but expressed in a more polemical way; this essence, too, is to be safeguarded by historical criticism. His polemical tone is not the expression of a scepticism which relativizes everything, but is meant to free theology from what Troeltsch believes to have become unimportant to it. The superiority of Christianity arises out of a historical insight: Christianity is superior because it loosed men and women from their ties to nature and freed them for reason and culture.

Nowadays we read Troeltsch, too, in a different situation, but he also raises questions worth remembering.

– If on the one hand we do in fact work with the three principles of
criticism, analogy and correlation which Troeltsch mentions, and on
the other hand no longer share his presupposition that history has a
meaning and a goal, are we left with any more than historical
relativism?

– If faith and reason can no longer be connected as trust in the rationality
of history and human beings, then do faith and actual historical work
fall so far apart that they can no longer be related?

2.4.2.3   Wrede

Troeltsch's requirements for theology generally were specifically related
to New Testament theology by William Wrede (1859-1906; after 1893
Professor in Breslau), in his programmatic article 'The Task and
Methods of "New Testament Theology"', which first appeared in 1897.

There is an English translation in Robert Morgan (ed.), *The Nature of New
Testament Theology*, SBT II 25, SCM Press 1973, 68-116.

Wrede, too, is concerned with more than a purely methodological
discussion, 'for New Testament theology is decisive for the question of
the essence and emergence of original Christianity' (68), and thus
for the question of Christianity generally. Like Troeltsch, Wrede
presupposes 'that New Testament theology must be considered and
done as a purely historical discipline' (69), and in particular he detaches
it from a pre-existing dogmatics, including a normative concept of the
canon.

For Wrede that excludes any account of New Testament theology -
as was usual in his time – based on the method of 'doctrinal concepts'
(73-84). Its place is to be taken by a structure derived from the history
of religion: 'the discipline has to lay out the history of early Christian
religion and theology' (84), with a stress on history, but also specifically
so that it is concerned not only with the content of scriptures, but also
with their concern: 'In the last resort, we at least want to know what
was believed, thought, taught, hoped, required and striven for in the
earliest period of Christianity' (109).

In the last part of his article, Wrede sketches out how he conceives
of such a theology of the New Testament as 'early Christian history of
religion' or 'the history of early Christian religion and theology' (116).
He himself never carried out this programme, but the division which
he proposes is familiar to us from present-day theologies of the New
Testament: Jesus – the faith of earliest Christianity, divided into 'the
Jewish-Christian early community and Christianity on heathen soil'

(106, see 2.3.3 on the view of history in the history-of-religions school) – Paul and his influence on Gentile Christianity – John.

However, an understanding of early Christianity and the history of its religion also include a knowledge of 'late Jewish theology': 'Judaism, not the Old Testament, is the basis of Christianity in the history of religion' (114). Unlike Deissmann (see 2.3.3), he will not accord 'Graeco-Roman paganism' such a status (115).

The decisive feature of Wrede's programme is the demand to make New Testament exegesis, including the theology of the New Testament, independent of dogmatics; to undertake a strictly historical account without taking account of the needs of dogma. This will be less a historical account of particular theologies of early Christianity as the development in the history of religions from 'late Judaism' via Jesus, the earliest community and Paul, to Gentile Christianity, especially as (according to Wrede) this is represented by the Gospel of John.

Wilhelm Bousset was the first to implement this approach for christology in his book *Kyrios Christos*, which appeared in 1913 and then in a second edition in 1921: christology as the work of the Gentile-Christian community, taking up Hellenistic conceptions of redemption (the book was reprinted with a foreword by Rudolf Bultmann in 1967 and translated into English: Abingdon Press 1970).

Wrede's programme is still influential today, first of all – as I have said – in the way in which the historical structure of a theology of the New Testament which it proposes has become established, although with modifications in individual details. Secondly, the question of the earliest Christian community, which already arises here, is worked out less in terms of the individual figures of early Christianity and more in those of form criticism (3.2.3).

However, questions remain:
– If such a development within early Christianity can be traced by historians, how far is it binding on theology and the church today?
– Does the detachment of New Testament exegesis from dogmatics in Wrede and in Troeltsch and Harnack represent a complete absence of presuppositions or does it create new ones?

2.4.2.4   Schweitzer

Lastly, it remains to mention Albert Schweitzer (1875-1965). He began as a New Testament scholar (a junior lecturer in Strasbourg in 1902) and also made himself a name as an organist and Bach scholar. However, it was as the doctor of Lambarene in the primeval forest that he became famous. As a New Testament scholar he could be said to come nearest to the history-of-religions school, as he, too, used newly-discovered apocalytic as a framework for the interpretation of the New Testament. His *The Quest of the Historical Jesus*, to use its familiar English title, was first published in 1906 as *From Reimarus to Wrede*, and after the second edition of 1913 was given the title *History of Research into the Life of Jesus*; it is a criticism of the attempts to ground Christianity in the historical Jesus made since the Enlightenment.

The English translation was made from the first edition and published in 1910. The third edition (A. & C.Black 1954, reissued SCM Press 1981) includes a new introduction written by Schweitzer in 1950, but unfortunately was never revised to take into account material added after the first edition. For this see D.E.Nineham, 'Schweitzer Revisited', *Explorations in Theology* 1, SCM Press 1977, 112-33.

Harnack had already asserted in a Habilitation thesis in 1874 that the source material did not allow the writing of a life of Jesus as a scientific biography (*Vita Jesu scribi nequit*), yet he could find the essence of Christianity in the historical Jesus (see 2.4.2.1). Schweitzer now shows that all attempts at such a life of Jesus fail to do justice to the historical Jesus – with the one exception of Reimarus (1694-1768), a selection of whose works Lessing had published in 1774-1778 as 'Fragments by an anonymous author'. By contrast, all the rest had merely read into the account of Jesus what they themselves wanted to claim as Christianity, Harnack included (see Schweitzer's verdict in 2.4.2.1).

The real Jesus was the alien Jesus, the other, apocalyptic Jesus, rooted in his time and no longer capable of being communicated to modern times. The last chapter of Schweitzer's book contains an impressive description of this alien Jesus: 'The study of the life of Jesus has had a curious history. It set out in quest of the historical Jesus, believing that when it had found him it could bring him straight into our time as a teacher and saviour' (397). 'He returned to his own time, not owing to the application of any historical ingenuity, but by the same inevitable necessity by which the liberated pendulum returns to its original position' (ibid.).

'Jesus means something to our world because a mighty spiritual force streams forth from him and flows through our time also. This fact can neither be shaken nor confirmed by any historical discovery' (397).

And the book ends almost mystically: 'He comes to us as One unknown, without a name, as of old, by the lake-side, he came to those men who knew him not. He speaks to us the same word: "Follow thou me!" and sets us to the tasks which he has to fulfil for our time. He commands. And to those who obey Him, whether they be wise or simple, he will reveal himself in the toils, the conflict, the sufferings which they shall pass through in his fellowship, and, as an ineffable mystery, they shall learn in their own experience who he is...'(401). The three points at the end of the book (which are not reproduced in the English translation) show that it is no longer possible to formulate this experience.

So here finally a legitimation of theology and church from the historical Jesus is disputed. What remain are impulses which emanated from Jesus and are still at work in the present, but which cannot be controlled by the historical Jesus because he expected the end of the world and did not see shaping it as his task.

Questions that remain are:
– What is the relationship between the Jesus who can be described in historical terms and Christianity, if evidently it is no longer possible to legitimate Christianity directly in the historical Jesus?
– How far is the question of shaping the world, which is also pressing for Schweitzer, a legitimate task of Christianity?

2.4.3   Aporias

The very different positions of Harnack, Troeltsch, Wrede and Schweitzer have in common the fact that each in his own way asks what is the original essence of Christianity in the form of a historical question, diverging in various polemical ways from traditional dogmatics. This question is focussed on christology, i.e. on the significance of Jesus of Nazareth for today, and is no longer answered within the framework of the doctrine of the two natures but in historical and psychological terms; Jesus is no longer 'true man and true God' in the metaphysical sense of the old confessions, but as the true man he is divine, the human ideal.

However, it becomes increasingly more questionable whether such a definition of the original essence of Christianity does justice to the historical Jesus, and at the same time whether a Christianity which is grounded in the historical Jesus is viable for the time around 1900. Friedrich Naumann's shift from a politics orientated on the Sermon on the Mount to the politics of a great power (such as the German Reich) orientated on 'political constraints' is an instructive example here (see H.Timm, *Friedrich Naumann's theologischer Widerruf*, Theologisches Existenz heute 141, 1967).

Historical theology came to an end around 1900 since it could no longer achieve its real concern, namely the historical verification of Christianity. All the attempts described here can be understood only as criticism of traditional dogmatics; they are not a fundamental questioning of Christianity, like the criticism of religion by Feuerbach or Marx.

A new and more radical approach to the problems of history and christology which are interrelated in the theme of the 'historical Jesus' was needed, but at the same time the results and open questions of historical theology continued to shape the subsequent period. The range of historical methods created in the nineteenth century remains, as do the results of exegetical research into basic questions; above all the question remains of the original and authentic essence of Christianity, given the way in which dogmatics is drawn into the morass of historical relativity.

3   Theological Exegesis

3.1   The claim of the Word of God: dialectical theology

3.1.1   Barth's *Romans*

The new exegetical approach was first of all marked by the work of an outsider; in 1919 a book appeared with the title *The Epistle to the Romans*; its author was a Swiss country pastor. Though not unknown in Germany, he came from the circle of liberal theologians and for a while was editor of their journal *Die Christliche Welt* (The Christian World). His name was Karl Barth (1886-1968), and he had none of the usual academic qualifications, not even a doctorate. His book was a commentary on the letter to the Romans: the letter is interpreted section by section and verse by verse, not with critical detachment, but in order to appropriate its thought.

The first edition was never translated. The famous English translation by Sir Edwyn Hoskyns was made from the second edition of 1922, which was very different from the first.
For the background see Eberhard Busch, *Karl Barth. His life from letters and autobiographical texts*, SCM Press and Fortress Press 1975, 92ff.

The preface to the first edition already mentions this purpose. 'Paul, as a child of his age, addressed his contemporaries. It is, however, far more important that, as prophet amd apostle of the kingdom of God, he veritably speaks to all men of every age. The differences between then and now, there and here, no doubt require careful investigation and consideration. But the purpose of such investigation can only be to demonstrate that these differences are, in fact, purely trivial... What was once of grave importance, is so still. What is today of grave importance – and not merely crotchety and incidental – stands in direct connexion with that ancient gravity. If we rightly understand ourselves, our problems are the problems of Paul; and if we are enlightened by the brightness of his answers, those answers must be ours' (1).
In the preface to the second edition, which appeared in 1922, Barth,

who had already been arguing with critics, goes over to the attack in defending his own approach to the text.

'I have, it is true, protested against recent commentaries on the Epistle to the Romans... But I have nothing whatever to say against historical criticism. I recognize it, and once more state quite definitely that it is both necessary and justified. My complaint is that recent commentators confine themselves to an interpretation of the text which seems to me to be no commentary at all, but merely the first step towads a commentary. Recent commentaries contain no more than a reconstruction of the text, a rendering of the Greek words and phrases by their precise equivalents, a number of additional notes in which archaeological and philological material is gathered together, and a more or less plausible arrangement of the subject matter in such a manner that it may be made historically and psychologically intelligible from the standpoint of pure pragmatism' (6).

'The critical historian needs to be more critical. The interpretation of what is written requires more than a disjointed series of notes on words and phrases. The commentator must be possessed of a wider intelligence than that which moves within the boundaries of his own natural appreciation. True apprehension can be achieved only by a strict determination to face, as far as possible without rigidity of mind, the tension displayed more or less clearly in the ideas written in the text' (8).

And he points to his own situation: 'I myself know what it means year in year out to mount the steps of the pulpit, conscious of the responsibility to understand and to interpret, and longing to fulfil it; and yet, utterly incapable, because at the university I had never been brought beyond that well-known "awe in the presence of history" which means in the end no more than that all hope of engaging in the dignity of understanding and interpretation has been surrendered' (9).

In Barth the historical distance between then and now and the distance between text and interpreter is replaced by the qualitative distance between God and the human being: and the question of truth in the New Testament texts is no longer 'What can still be valid?' but 'What was valid?' Precisely that which was pushed on one side by historical criticism as being alien now becomes what is authentic. The identity between kingdom of God and culture is also challenged; the literature referred to is no longer the classics, but Dostoievsky, Tolstoy and Kierkegaard.

Above all, however, Barth takes up radical nineteenth-century criticism of religion: Nietzsche, Feuerbach, Overbeck. With them religion is denounced as human, but is now also condemned theologically as godlessness. The Word of God emerges in the face of all such human religion as the revelation of the judgment of God on all that is human. Finally, the problem of history, the main theme of historical theology, is transcended, in that God is understood as the negation of history: the resurrection of Jesus as the brutal incursion of God into the world and history. Theology, which is now resolutely orientated on the New Testament, thus has a high degree of alienation from the world, of distance from the world, from society, politics and culture.

That must be seen against the background of the situation after the First World War, the end of which was experienced in a great variety of cultural and scientific circles in Germany as a collapse, but one which at the same time could lead to a completely new beginning – in connection with the exegesis of the New Testament. What proved to be aporias at the end of historical theology (see 2.4) could now be seen more radically – more critically – than by historical criticism.

3.1.2   Bultmann's theology of the existence of human beings before God

3.1.2.1   Bultmann's move towards theological exegesis

The professional exegetes largely shook their heads over Barth's *Romans*, and at best benevolently dismissed the book as a piece of original practical exegesis.

Cf. above all the review by Adolf Jülicher, reprinted in James M.Robinson (ed.), *The Beginnings of Dialectical Theology*, John Knox Press 1968, 72-81. The review by Bultmann referred to below is on pp.100-20.

So there was astonishment when a professional, Rudolf Bultmann (1884-1976), for all his detailed criticism, accepted this kind of exegesis 'against the psychologizing and historicizing view of religion' (100): 'In the understanding of the task of explaining the text as Barth develops in the Foreword, I am quite in agreement with him. As it is self-evident for him that the philological-historical explanation of the text is a necessary side of exegesis, it is self-evident for me that a text can be explained only when one has an inner relationship to the matter with which the text deals' (118).

Bultmann came from the circle of the history-of-religions group (see 2.3.3); his main teachers had been J.Weiss and W.Heitmüller, and also Gunkel in Berlin (see 3.2.2). He gained his doctorate in Marburg with a work on 'The Style of Pauline Preaching and the Cynic-Stoic Diatribe', a topic characteristic of history-of-religions exegesis, and this appeared as a book the same year; his Habilitationsschrift, which was not published until 1984, was on a historical topic related to exegesis: 'The Exegesis of Theodore of Mopsuestia' (a church father born in 428 who belonged to the Antiochene school, a trend which advocated a philological interpetation of the Bible). After teaching at Breslau and Giessen Bultmann returned to Marburg in 1921. This was the year in which his *The History of the Synoptic Tradition* (see 3.2.2) appeared; it, too, shows his origins in the history-of-religions school.

3.1.2.2   Liberal and dialectical theology

In 1924, Bultmann justified the attitude he had taken in 1922 in his review of *Romans*, in an article on 'Liberal Theology and the Latest Theological Movement', a movement which was later identified with the term 'dialectical theology'.

There is an English translation in his *Faith and Understanding*, London and New York 1969, 28-52.

Bultmann begins by saying that 'the attack against the so-called liberal theology is not to be understood as a repudiation of its own past, but as a discussion with the past. The new movement is not a revival of orthodoxy, but rather a carefully reasoned consideration of the consequences which have resulted from the situation brought about by liberal theology' (28). The theme of the controversy is: 'The subject of theology is God, and the chief charge to be brought against liberal theology is that it has dealt not with God but with man' (29).

Bultmann carries on this polemical discussion under two of the headings established in liberal theology: history (Part 1) and ethics (Part 2). First he evaluates positively as a contribution of liberal theology 'the development of the critical sense, that is, freedom and veracity' (29). But its course took such a direction (see 2.4) that it could no longer be grounded in a historical picture of Jesus. However – and this is Bultmann's accusation – it did not recognize this radically enough.

From that follows its second mistake, that 'no objection was made to the inclusion of the person of Jesus in the complex of general historical inter-relations. Indeed, it was acceptable as theology because of the belief that the revelation of God in history could be perceived precisely within this nexus of relations' (3.2 – see especially Troeltsch, 2.4.2.2). Bultmann lays this charge against the term 'pantheism of history' (32), by which he means that just as pantheism felt that it could experience divine powers in nature, so liberal theology thought that it could experience divine powers in history which bring human beings from their natural state to culture: 'In these powers... lies the meaning of history, its divine character. God reveals himself in human personalities who are the bearers of these powers. And Jesus, so far as he is also in this sense a personality, is the bearer of revelation' (34).

Over against this, Bultmann says, 'Truly, here, too, it is only man that is deified; for the human powers are alleged to be divine', and there is no recognition that 'the Word of God is judgment upon the whole nature and condition of man' (35); 'all of them totally lack the insight that God is other than the world, he is beyond the world, and that this means the complete abrogation of the whole man, of his whole history. Their common aim is to give faith the kind of basis which destroys the very essence of faith, because what they seek is a basis here in this world' (40) – that corresponds to Barth's understanding of faith as a 'vacuum' which cannot in any way be defined in terms of psychology and experience.

So the charge is levelled specifically against the identification of God and history, which comes to a head in the christological question as to how far the Jesus of Nazareth described by liberal theology as 'true man' could be divine. The aporias which had been most clearly described by Albert Schweitzer (see 2.4.2.4) were to be overcome by a new understanding of history which Bultmann sketches out in the introductory section of his book *Jesus and the Word* (first published in 1926; English translation 1934, reissued Fontana Books 1958): not to give evaluations with the critical detachment of the historian who apparently stands above history, but to enter into a dialogue with it as one involved in history.

Jesus and the Word is itself a controversial work directed against liberal theology. Its structure clearly follows Harnack's *What is Christianity?* (see 2.4.2.1) by being in three sections, and the argument with Harnack can also be traced down to points of detail, though Harnack is never mentioned by name (the book does not in fact contain any explicit quotations).

For Bultmann, over against Harnack's Jesus there now stands the alien Jesus, and Bultmann's book is not primarily a description of the essence of Christianity; on the contrary, Bultmann does not define this essence in terms of the historical Jesus but rather in terms of the kerygma (see 3.2.3); remarkably enough, however, this consequence is not even mentioned anywhere. As *Jesus and the Word* appeared in Germany in a series which bore the title 'The Immortals', it could certainly hae been read in its time in the same way as Harnack's *What is Christianity?*, but the Christianity it presented would seem very alien.

In the second part of the article on the relationship between dialectical and liberal theology, Bultmann discusses the theme of ethics first by

arguing against the view that 'our secular daily work in the place assigned
to us in history is service to God' (40); this is false 'when it is assumed
that labour in every kind of occupation is in itself direct service to God;
when it is forgotten that my activity in my own occupation can separate
me from God and become service to idols' (41).

He describes as characteristic of liberal theology the view that 'specific
ideals for the activity of life in the world are to be derived from faith.
That is to say, that Christian concepts of the kingdom of God, of love,
et al., can determine man's life within the world, that they can provide
the norm, setting the goal and showing the road to it. The consequences
of this view are clear in such slogans as "the work of God's kingdom",
"the vineyard of God on earth", "Christian Socialism", "Christianity
and Pacifism"' (42). Against this Bultmann says: 'No act exists which
can relate itself directly to God and his kingdom' (42). 'There is service
of God only where man surrenders himself to God's judgment and then
obediently under God takes up the work in the world to which God has
set him, when he never averts his eyes from the sin of the world –
especially not from his own sins – and never dreams that any sort of
approximation to God's world can be realized in this world... certainly
the behaviour of the man of faith (if the existence of men of faith may
be assumed) will appear different from that of the unbeliever. But in
what respects it will differ cannot be deduced from his faith. He will
learn the difference through his obedience when he takes upon himself
service in this world with the responsibilities and the duties which are
realities in this world and for this world' (44f.)

As in Barth, this is a complete rejection of any attempt to shape the
world in Christian terms, and this comes about by radicalizing liberal
theology itself: 'Who has emphasized more forcibly than W. Herrmann
that there is no specifically Chrisitan ethic? And who has shown more
convincingly than Troeltsch the problematic character of the relation
of the Christian to the world?' (45).

In the third part of the article Bultmann describes the opposite
position to liberal theology by asking: 'What conception of God and
man forms the basis for this criticism of liberal theology?' (45). His first
reply is: 'God represents the total annulment of man, his negation,
calling him in question, indeed judging him' (46). 'The knowledge of
this truth is called faith. Faith cannot generate itself in man; it can only
arise as man's answer to the Word of God in which God's judgment and
God's grace are preached to him' (47). Theology is the explication of
this faith: 'The subject of theology is God. Theology speaks of God
because it speaks of man as he stands before God. That is, theology
speaks out of faith' (52).

So in Bultmann, as in Barth, this new theological beginning does not mean a departure from historical criticism; rather, that criticism is made more radical. The aporias discovered by historical criticism, particularly in the question of the historical Jesus, remain and are even used as a criticism of historical criticism. They cannot be resolved or played out, but open up a way to the real aporia, the position of men and women before God.

3.1.2.3   Theological exegesis of the New Testament

Bultmann sketches out how exegesis of the New Testament is to be done in the light of this new approach in his 1925 article 'The Problem of a Theological Exegesis of the New Testament'.

English translation in James M.Robinson (ed.), *The Beginnings of Dialectical Theology*, John Knox Press 1968, 236-56.

Bultmann expresses the difference from historical theology in the formula: 'Historical exegesis asks: "What is said?" We ask "What is meant?" ' (239); there is no longer neutral detachment from the text but the claim of the text on its readers. The truth-question is now: 'What does it mean for me and how am I to understand it on its objective ground?'(239) Bultmann then takes the difference between 'said' and 'meant' further, to the point of rejecting 'neutral' exegesis: 'There is no bare interpretation of "what is there", but in some way (a specific way, in fact, for each case) the interpretation of the text always goes hand in hand with the exegete's interpretation of himself' (242). He rejects the charge of subjectivism with the counter-charge that even any apparently objective method 'is merely an approach that is the consequence of the underlying interpretation of human existence' (244).

The leading question in exegesis of the text is now: 'We attempt to understand the way in which the text shows its writer's interpretation of his concept of existence as the real possibility of existing' (248). According to Bultmann, at the same time that is the task of theology generally: 'For theology is the conceptual presentation of man's existence as an existence determined by God' (252).

It follows from this that: 'Since textual interpretation cannot be separated from self-interpretation, and self-interpretation becomes explicit in New Testament exegesis, and since, on the other hand, the self-interpretation of man as a historical individual can occur only in the interpretation of history, the result is that theology and exegesis – or systematic and historical theology – fundamentally coincide' (253).

As the 'task of conceptual thinking' (253), theology is to be distinguished from the proclamation of the Word: the task of exegetical theology is a New Testament theology, with the stress on theology, not the history of earliest Christianity, as it is in Wrede (see 2.4.2.3). Its form would be expressed pointedly in the production of a lexicon of the history of words; here is a second strand which entered the *Theological Dictionary of the New Testament* (*TDNT*, see 2.3.3), for the first volume of which Bultmann in fact wrote a series of articles: 'It includes the grammatical task, as well as all research into concepts and the history of religion' (256).

This view of theology as a conceptual explication of theology also explains why in his *Theology of the New Testament* (which appeared in Germany in three volumes between 1948 and 1953 and in England in two volumes in 1952 and 1955) Bultmann speaks of theology only in connection with Paul and John, whereas both the proclamation of Jesus and the kerygma of the primitive community and the Hellenistic community appear as 'presuppositions and motives of New Testament theology'. The view that christology is not really theology but proclamation ('kerygma') is also based on this understanding of theology.

The continuity between Bultmann and historical theology, especially the history-of-religions school, will become particularly evident when we consider form criticism; however, it can also be seen in the picture of the history of early Christianity which is taken over from there (see 2.3.3) and in the interpretation of the New Testament in terms of the model of the Gnostic myth (see 2.3.3). However, for Bultmann form criticism, which in itself has a sociological and aesthetic orientation (see 3.2.2), becomes the basic theological questioning of the Jesus tradition. In the historical picture the differentiation of the Hellenistic community from Paul becomes the difference between kerygma and theology. Finally, Gnosticism no longer serves to provide a derivation for statements in the New Testament, but particularly in Bultmann's *Commentary on John* (see 2.3.2) becomes a model of interpretation in that here the questions of truth which occupy human beings at all times become evident. Thus Gnosticism is not an interchangeable model from the history of religions but is part of theology itself, as the formulation of the human questions and desires to which revelation is the answer.

3.1.2.4   Existentialist interpretation

Finally, continuity and argumentation with historical theology can be seen once again in the programme of demythologizing which Bultmann set out in 1941 in his article 'New Testament and Theology'.

For a long time the only available, rather free, English translation was in

Kerygma and Myth, London 1952; there is now a new translation by Schubert M.Ogden in *New Testament and Mythology*, London and Philadelphia 1985 (to which the page references are given).

Demythologizing 'is not a new task at which theology today is the first to work. On the contrary, everything which has been said up to this point, or something like it, could have been said thirty or forty years ago, and it is really a *testimonium paupertatis* for our theological situation that it has to be said again today' (11). The problem is that not only the picture of the world in the New Testament but also its account of the saving event is mythical: 'the individual motifs may be easily traced to the contemporary mythology of Jewish apocalyptic and of the Gnostic myth of redemption. Insofar as it is mythological talk it is incredible to men and women today because for them the mythical world picture is a thing of the past' (2f.).

A series of abrupt sentences using the term 'is finished' (belief in spirit and demons, the New Testament miracles, eschatology) argues from the picture of the world produced by the natural sciences, but this is not just any arbitrary picture of the world; it shapes the whole context in which we live, because the world has been shaped by the natural sciences and technology.

Bultmann sees the legitimation of the task of demythologizing in some characteristics of myth: 'The real point of myth is not to give an objective world picture; what is expressed in it, rather, is how we human beings understand the world. Thus, myth does not want to be interpreted in cosmological terms but in anthropological terms – or better, in existentialist terms' (9). Here for the Gnostic myth he refers particularly to the interpretation by Hans Jonas (he was not afraid to mention this Jewish scholar even in 1941).

Hans Jonas, *Gnosis und spätantiker Geist*, I. *Die mythologische Gnosis*, FRLANT 51, 1934 (cf. the dedication and preface to Part II.1 of the same work, FRLANT 63, 1954).

What is true of myth generally is also true of the New Testament: 'For this reason the mythology of the New Testament, also, is not to be questioned with respect to the content of its objectifying representations but with respect to the understanding of existence that expresses itself in them. What is at issue is the truth of this understanding, and the faith that affirms its truth is not to be bound to the New Testament's world of representations' (10). In addition, in the case of the New Testament, 'some of its representations are mutually disharmonious and, in fact, contradictory' and 'a particular contradiction... runs throughout the New Testament:... human beings are understood, on the one hand, as cosmic beings and, on the other hand, as independent persons who can win or lose themselves by their own decisions' (11).

'If we may say schematically that during the epoch of critical research the mythology of the New Testament was simply eliminated, the task today – also to speak schematically – is to interpret New Testament mythology' (12).

Alongside this argument with historical theology there is a second argument which was to make the programme of demythologizing the topic of such vigorous discussion: 'If for the last twenty years we have been called back from criticism to simple acceptance of the New Testament kerygma, theology and the church have run the risk of uncritically repristinating New Testament mythology, thereby making the kerygma unintelligible for the present. The critical work of earlier generations cannot be simply thrown away but must be positively appropriated. If this does not happen, sooner or later – provided church and theology continue to exist at all – the old battles between orthodoxy and liberalism will have to be fought all over again' (11f.).

The clause in parentheses refers to the situation of the Confessing Church in the Third Reich. Whereas German Protestantism on the whole took a more tentative attitude, Bultmann, like Barth from the beginning, saw 'that we have to decide whether Christian faith is to be valid for us or not... It is a matter of either-or.' That is the way in which the lectures with which he began the 1933 summer semester ended on 2 May 1933; he had the text published just a month later.

R. Bultmann, 'Die Aufgabe der Theologie in der gegenwärtigen Situation', *Theologische Blätter* 12, 1933, 161-6.

Now, in 1941, Bultmann was at the same time asking what the Confessing Church had to confess; he was asking what Christian faith was, and how its proclamation could be related to the present.

In the second part of the demythologizing programme Bultmann outlined the basic features of such demythologizing as 'existentialist interpretation', as it was required by myth itself and thus also by the New Testament itself – it was not detached historical interpretation. Existentialist interpretation meant: 'Is there in such talk a view of human existence that offers even to us today, who no longer think mythologically, a possibility for understanding ourselves?'(15). 'Existentialist' denotes basic conditions of human life like anxiety, hope, transitoriness, etc., which as such are timeless and transcend the individual and thus create bridges of understanding between then and now: historical distance is transcended and done away with in the identity of human existence.

The term 'existentialist' is to be distinguished from 'existential', which relates to the way in which the individual is affected by such existentialia, i.e. anxiety, hope, etc. in particular concrete forms.

Bultmann sees the Christian self-understanding characterized by the fact that ' "this world" is the world of transience and death' (16). 'Transience and death are traced back... to sin' (27). 'Paul sees that human life is burdened with "care" (I Cor.7.32ff.). Everyone cares about something. By nature our care is directed toward securing our life. "We put confidence in the flesh" (Phil.3.3-4), depending on our possibilities and successes in the sphere of what is visible, and consciousness of our security finds expression in "boasting". This attitude is incongruous, however, given our actual situation, for we are not really secure at all' (16f.).

'What is visible and disposable is transient, and consequently whoever lives on the basis of it falls subject to transience and death. Whoever lives out of what can be disposed of is given over to dependence on it... Out of this also grows the slavery of anxiety that oppresses all of us (Rom.8.15) – the anxiety in which we each seek to hold on to ourselves and what is ours in the secret feeling that everything, including our own life, is slipping away from us' (16f.).

How can human beings get out of this complex of disaster? 'By contrast, a genuine human life would be one in which we lived out of what is invisible and non-disposable and, therefore, surrendered all self-contrived security. This is life "according to the Spirit" or life "in faith". Such a life becomes a possibility for us through faith in God's "grace", that is, through trust that precisely what is invisible, unfamiliar, and nondisposable encounters us as love, gives us our future, means life for us and not death' (17).

The existentialist interpretation of the dogmatic terms grace and faith are made more precise in further identifications: 'The grace of God is the grace that forgives sin, that is, it frees us from our past, which holds us in bondage' (17f.).

'They who open themselves in grace receive the forgiveness of sin, that is, become free from the past, and just this is what is meant by "faith": to open ourselves freely to the future' (18).

'Such faith is simultaneously obedience, because it is our turning away from ourselves, our surrendering all security, our renouncing any attempt to be acceptable, to gain our life, to trust in ourselves, and our resolving to trust solely in God who raises the dead (II Cor.1.9) and who calls into existence the things that do not exist (Rom.4.17). It is radical submission to God, which expects everything from God and nothing from ourselves; and it is the release thereby given from everything in the world that can be disposed of, and hence the attitude of being free from the world, of freedom' (18).

The prevalence of negative terms is striking here (words denoting surrender, renunciation, being given release, and hence 'freedom'), and so Christian freedom is also characterized as 'a distance from the world for which all participation in things worldly takes place in the attitude of *as if not* (*hōs mē*; I Cor.7.29-31).' (18) This *hōs mē* and the Pauline text cited with it become the basic model of the Christian relation to the world: not shaping the world but detached freedom from the world.

Moreover eschatology of an apocalyptic or a Gnostic kind and the understanding of Spirit as a power which works through nature are also interpreted in existentialist terms. Christian eschatology means neither an impending cosmic event (thus apocalyptic) nor a life outside this world (thus Gnosticism) but the presence of salvation, albeit under conditions of this world: 'the decision of faith is not made once and for all but must be confirmed in each concrete situation by being made anew' (19). And 'spirit' does not mean a realization of the divine within the world in the form of ecstasy or miracles, 'it is rather the possibility of life that one must lay hold of by resolve' (20).

Thus according to Bultmann what is said mythologically in the New Testament is meant in existentialist terms: the making possible of a life in this world which is free from this world. But the programme of demythologizing also carries out what in 1924 Bultmann had named as the theme of theology: 'The subject of theology is God, and theology talks of God by talking of human beings as they are before God, i.e. in the light of faith' (3.1.2.2). The description of the Christian understanding of being matches this demand. There remains (and this is the main theme of the whole article) the question what significance christology has, 'whether the Christian understanding of being can be realized without Christ' (31). This theme inevitably arises from different sides:

– If the foundation of Christianity is no longer the historical Jesus but proclamation of him, how can this proclamation be demythologized in such a way that something remains in it which can be said to be specifically Christian?

– If, and Bultmann knew this as well as his critics, this account of the Christian understanding of being comes very close to what has been developed in Karl Jaspers' philosophy of existence and especially by Martin Heidegger as existentialist analysis of human being, is it not an understanding of being which is not specifically Christian as such, and above all is not directed towards revelation?

Bultmann is right, first, in putting the second question, in that the issue is not a matter of 'whether human nature could have been discovered without the New Testament. Of course, as a matter of fact it has not been discovered without the New Testament; there would not be any modern philosophy without the New Testament, without Martin Luther, without Kierkegaard' (25). But this is just a superficial connection in cultural history and does not touch on the real question 'whether our "nature" as human beings can be realized, that is, whether we are already brought to ourselves simply in being shown what our authentic "nature" is (or in reflecting on it ourselves)' (25).

This question about ethical practice which can first be heard in 'realized' cannot be answered in the affirmative by Bultmann, as that would amount to self-realization; hence the further definition, 'that is', and the passive formulation of the definition ('are brought'). So the decision is not made in the sphere of ethics, but: 'This, then is the decisive point that distinguishes the New Testament from philosophy, Christian faith from "natural" self-understanding: the New Testament talks and Christian faith knows about an act of God that first makes possible our submission, our faith, our love, our authentic life' (31).

So the problem comes to a head over the first question, that about christology and the kerygma, over the question 'whether we here stand before a myth or before an event that has a mythical character... The question remains whether the claim that the transition from the first kind of existence to the second, our liberation from ourselves for our own authentic life, is conceivable only as an act of God, and that faith can be actual only as faith in the love of God revealed in Christ' (31f.). And this remains the question if demythologizing is also applied to the New Testament proclamation: 'The question that concerns us now is whether the event in which the New Testament sees the act of God, the revelation of God's love, namely, the Christ occurrence, is a mythical event' (32).

The starting point is that 'the Christ occurrence is not a myth like the cult myths of the Greek or Hellenistic gods. The Jesus Christ who is God's son, a pre-existent divine being, is at the same time a certain historical person, Jesus of Nazareth; and his destiny as a person is not only a mythical occurrence but at the same time a human destiny that ends with crucifixion. The historical and the mythical here are peculiarly intertwined' (32). As earlier the retreat to ethical realization was excluded, so here is a retreat to the historical Jesus – according to Bultmann that would be an elimination of the mythical and thus the way of historical theology.

As a working hypothesis, Bultmann's thesis is framed as a question: 'Thus the question becomes pressing whether the point of such mythological talk is not simply to express the significance of the historical figure of Jesus and his story, namely their significance as saving figure and salvation occurrence. If this were their point, their content as objectifying representations could be given up' (41).

This is relatively easy for Bultmann in the case of statements about
the pre-existence of Christ and the Virgin Birth: 'What he is for us is
not exhausted by, in fact, does not even appear in, what he seems to be
for ordinary historical observation. We are not to ask about his historical
origin, because his real meaning becomes evident only when this way
of asking questions is set aside. We are not to ask for the historical
reasons for his story, his cross; the significance of his story lies in what
God wants to say to us through it' (33).

Thus 'everything is concentrated in the chief question about cross
and resurrection' (33). In the New Testament the cross of Jesus, too, is
not simply depicted as historical event, but is raised up to cosmic
dimensions. However, its significance is interpreted in existentialist
terms: 'By allowing Jesus to be crucified God has established the cross
for us. Thus, to believe in the cross of Christ does not mean to look to
some mythical process that has taken place outside of us and our world
or at an objectively visible event that God has somehow reckoned to
our credit; rather, to believe in the cross of Christ means to accept the
cross as one's own and to allow oneself to be crucified with Christ' (34).
'Thus, Christ's cross and sufferings are present' (35), and not just
historical past. 'As the salvation occurrence, then, the cross of Christ
is not a mythical event but a historical occurrence that has its origin in
the historical event of the crucifixion of Jesus of Nazareth. In its
historical significance this event is the judgment of the world, the
liberating judgment of us ourselves as human beings' (35). 'But this is
not at all the way in which the crucified one is proclaimed in the New
Testament, so that the point of the cross would be disclosed by his
historical life, which is to be reproduced by historical research. On the
contrary, he is proclaimed as the crucified one who is at the same time
the risen one. Cross and resurrection belong together as a unity' (36).

This brings the questioning to yet another point: 'But what about the
resurrection of Christ? Is it not an utterly mythical event? In any case,
it is not a historical event that is to be understood in its significance.
Can talking about Christ's resurrection be anything other than an
expression of the significance of the cross? Does it say anything else
than that Jesus' death on the cross is not to be seen as a human death
but rather as God's liberating judgment of the world, the judgment that
as such robs death of its power? Is it not precisely this truth that is
expressed by the statement that the crucified one is not dead but risen?'
(36). Putting the question in this way suggests an answer to the reader.

'The resurrection of Jesus cannot be an authenticating miracle on the
basis of which a doubter can be secure in believing in Christ... It is so
because the resurrection itself is an object of faith; and one cannot
secure one faith (faith in the saving meaning of the cross) by another

(faith in the resurrection)' (37f.) 'In fact, faith in the resurrection is nothing other than faith in the cross as the salvation event, as the cross of Christ' (39).

This faith does not arise out of a historical report, but out of proclamation, therefore: 'Christ the crucified and risen one encounters us in the word of proclamation, and nowhere else. And faith in this word is the true faith of Easter' (39).

In this conception the two basic problems of historical theology (history and ethics) are transcended: the kerygma proclaims the present significance of historical happening, which thus does not just remain past; the decision of faith in each case leads to proving faith in a specific situation in the present, but is not self-realization by means of ethical action. The demythologizing which is unconditionally called for by Bultmann is carried through consistently – apart for a possible mythological remnant, namely talk of an act of God (41). Here the question of the relationship with philosophy could ultimately remain open, if such talk of an act of God interpreted in existentialist terms meant only human decision. Bultmann avoids this consequence with a reference to the paradox 'that God's eschatological emissary is a concrete historical person, that God's eschatological act takes place in a human destiny, that it is an occurrence, therefore, that cannot be proved to be eschatological in any worldly way' (41). It remains a matter of faith, and cannot be grounded in an analysis of human beings and the world.

3.1.3 Revelation or existence?

The debate over Bultmann's programme of demythologizing was a particularly dominant feature of theological discussion in the 1950s. Here the ways of Barth and Bultmann, which had once again come together in the church struggle, finally parted: Bultmann accused Barth of simply ignoring the problem of mythological talk in the New Testament; Barth accused Bultmann of tying revelation to a particular philosophy. The gulf between them was unbridgeable.

Among the many questions and subsidiary questions touched on in this discussion, the following are particularly important:
– Is Bultmann's concept of myth and thus his stress on the contrasts between antiquity and modern times appropriate?
– Is Bultmann's concept of history and thus his bridging over of historical distances by human existence appropriate?
– Is the concept of the kerygma and with it the existentialist interpretation of cross and resurrection appropriate?
Above all, however, this once again raised the question of the 'essence

of Christianity', or better the question of the identity of Christian belief over and above its history.

3.2 The question of the community as the vehicle of the tradition: form criticism

3.2.1 The basic problem

The basic problem of form criticism lies in the insight that in the New Testament we are primarily dealing with texts, and not directly with the events which they report. These texts have been formulated in particular forms and for particular purposes, and not otherwise, and thus show a particular interest on the part of the one who narrates in this way; at the same time they reflect the expectations of those for whom they are written. Accordingly they are not formulated in neutral detachment from what they report, but indicate the commitment of both the author and his readers.

3.2.2 Aesthetic and sociological beginnings

With its close personal connections with the history-of-religions school (see 2.3.3), and like that school particularly stimulated by the Old Testament scholar Hermann Gunkel, form criticism also came into being as a corrective to literary criticism (see 2.2.3), which asked about historical sources and was not thought of as a mere supplement to literary criticism. Here too interest was no longer focussed on what was historically unique and underivable, but on the typical and universal features of early Christianity which were now to be discovered from the form and content of the texts. Here form criticism took up earlier beginnings above all in J.G.Herder (see 2.2.4) and German Romanticism (cf. e.g. the collection of folk tales by the Grimm brothers) with its interest in the discovery and collection not of 'great' literature but of the non-literary anonymous popular tradition which follows particular formal laws ('once upon a time'... 'and they lived happily ever after' are the way in which fairy tales begin and end, regardless of their particular content and setting). There was an aesthetic value judgment here in that it was the original, that which was not artificial, that was prized and sought after.

Cf. A.Jolles, *Einfache Formen*, 1930, ²1958, who investigates the typical formal elements in such forms as legends, sagas, riddles, jokes and so on.

Measured by the forms of great ('classical') literature like epic poetry, drama, dialogue and treatise, and measured by the concern for form and style of the individual author which can be recognized in any example of classical literature, the writings of the New Testament (the letters apart) simply represent minor literature which – as the church fathers already recognized – hardly lives up to any literary claims.

This is not so much because of their content, which – as the history of theology will show – can be depicted in large-scale forms, but because of the vehicles of the tradition and the way in which this tradition has been handed down. The synoptic Gospels can largely be broken down into very brief individual stories (as in fact also happens when they are used in lectionaries) which do not seem to require any knowledge of the context in order to be understood: the individual evangelists have put individual stories in quite different contexts. They are linked only by a loose juxtaposition with the help of very simple and indefinite pieces of information like 'and after that', 'now when he', 'and he came to', and so on. This was brought out in particular by K.L.Schmidt in his book *Der Rahmen der Geschichte Jesu* (The Framework of the Story of Jesus, 1919 reprinted 1964). In contrast to literary criticism and its interest, this meant that it is impossible to construct the biographical course of the activity of Jesus from the sequence of individual stories as we find it in the Gospels, as it is not intended to be chronological (except in the passion narratives).

These individual stories can be grouped according to particular formal characteristics, as they display the same elements in the same sequence, which are not just required by the course of action but arise out of the laws of narrative: for example in healing stories the description of the case and how difficult it is, the intervention of Jesus and the confirmation of his success either by a comment from the narrator or in the form of an astonished exclamation by the crowd. The real interest is directed towards Jesus as the healer, not to the person who is healed (we hear nothing about what happens to the latter).

Stories which describe Jesus' controversies with opponents ('disputes') begin with a description of the subject of the conflict, usually in the form of a question from these opponents, and end with an answer from Jesus which usually goes far beyond the specific instance and is formulated as a brief rule. Here too the real interest is in Jesus; he has the last word, and there is no interest in what his opponents thought of it.

All these stories have a large number of stereotypes: Jesus is always the only person to be mentioned by name; the others are usually 'the Pharisees', 'the disciples', 'the crowd', 'a sick person', 'many sick people'; there is no indication of the place or time of the event, or these are evident from the event itself (the stilling of the storm in Mark 4.36-41 must of course take place on 'the lake', and the controversy in Mark 6.1-6 of course in his home town, though the place-name Nazareth does not appear once in the text). This corresponds above all to a kind of oral narrative with no literary claims, as when one might be telling someone else: 'I came... he said to me... I said to her...' Where there are similarities with other literature from antiquity known to us, this too is minor literature.

Martin Dibelius (1883-1947) and Rudolf Bultmann (see 3.1.2), both pupils of the Old Testament scholar Hermann Gunkel (1862-1932), grouped and interpreted the narrative material and the discourse material in the synoptic Gospels independently of each other in this way and in essentials arrived at amazingly similar results.

Martin Dibelius, *From Tradition to Gospel*, Ivor Nicholson and Watson 1934, reissued James Clarke 1971;
Rudolf Bultmann, *The History of the Synoptic Tradition*, Blackwell and Harper and Row ²1968.

These books have remained standard works of synoptic exegesis down to the present day – more than sixty years after their first appearance – and have not been replaced by more recent works, which is amazing in view of the short life of so many other theological books.

There is a difference between them in method in so far as Dibelius begins more strictly from the form of the text and infers the 'setting in life' (*Sitz im Leben*) from it, whereas Bultmann defines the form more markedly from the content and, taking up the view of history in the history-of-religions school (see 2.3.3 and 3.1.2.3), is interested in the history of the tradition of the individual text from Jesus to the version we now have in the Gospels.

The term 'setting in life', introduced by Gunkel, denotes the functional setting of a form: where and for what purpose a particular form is used. In the case of the New Testament, this setting was within the early Christian community: worship, preaching, eucharist, baptismal instruction, etc.

Unlike Dibelius, Bultmann also passes judgment on whether a particular saying of Jesus can in fact be attributed historically to Jesus or not, but he then uses criteria which do not follow from form criticism itself (see 3.4.2), since by virtue of its approach form criticism can only get as far as those who hand down the tradition; 'setting in life' does not mean the situation in which Jesus uttered a particular saying but the situation in the Christian community in which such sayings of Jesus were used.

Texts from the Gospel of John appear in both writers in so far as they have contact with synoptic texts, i.e. above all the miracle stories. Only the passion narrative in the Gospel of John is discussed at any length, and the passion narratives of all the Gospels are special instances, in that here there is a major narrative complex which is not essentially an arbitrary sequence of events. However, this should not lead us astray so that we fail to notice that the Gospels nevertheless transpose the sequence of individual scenes and that here too typical figures predominate ('the high priest and scribes', 'the Sanhedrin'); the functions of places, times and persons stand in the foreground, not individual characteristics of persons or places.

The difference in method between Bultmann and Dibelius comes out particularly clearly in their discussion of the passion narratives. Dibelius asks how the narrative form 'passion narrative' ever came into being, and concludes from the theme of the fulfilment of scripture which can be found everywhere that this is a theological way of coping with the offence caused by the death of Jesus on the cross. So the 'setting in life' is preaching within the community. Here in particular: 'The point was to show that a paradoxical event, without human sense, represented the beginning of the Last Day, and was thus a part of the fulfilment of salvation' (185).

By contrast, Bultmann investigates the history of the origin of the passion narratives and sees the kerygma as their starting point (Mark 8.31; 9.31; 10.33f. and e.g. Acts 2.22-24): 'We have to reckon this kerygma as the earliest connected account of the passion and death of Jesus. But close to it,... was a short narrative of historical reminiscence about the arrest, condemnation and execution of Jesus' (275). The kerygma provides as it were the 'scarlet thread', and in Bultmann's view the short narrative will have been expanded and filled out with individual scenes or short connected passages. In thus investigating the earlier history of the tradition, Bultmann keeps closer to literary criticism than Dibelius, but without taking over its historical evaluations (see 2.2.3).

This difference also becomes clear in the way in which the logia source Q (see 2.2.4) is treated. Dibelius classifies it under the form 'paraenesis' and thus sees its 'setting in life' as ethical instruction; he dispenses with a literary-critical reconstruction of its extent, though he compares it with other ethical passages in the New Testament (233-6), Bultmann, however, again investigates the history of the tradition and assumes that Q was originally written in Aramaic and then translated into Greek, at which point some material from the tradition of the Hellenistic community was added (328).

3.2.3   The community as the place of the tradition

In contrast to literary criticism, which saw the texts of the Gospels as the sources from which one could reconstruct the historical events in the life of Jesus and show 'how it really was' (see 2.2.3), form criticism draws attention to the conditions under which the tradition was handed down and to those involved in the process, i.e. those who stand between the events reported and the Gospels as they are in their final form. In the Old Testament this question leads us to basic situations – the camp fire, the trial, the family and the cult – and Hermann Gunkel, the founder of form criticism, manifestly shows a high degree of aesthetic interest in his investigation.

In the New Testament, however, the investigation always brings us only to the context of the community (where, as in the parables, we find similar basic situations – peasants, shepherds, fishermen, etc. – these lie outside the sphere of form criticism!). This is because of the nature of the tradition, but it is also not unconnected with the revived interest of dialectical theology in the church as the context of theology.

Thus form criticism in effect became the theologically adequate way of raising questions. Both Dibelius (7) and Bultmann (4) repudiate aesthetic considerations, and describe the form-critical approach more as a sociological one. That does not mean that they base themselves on a particular sociological theory (at that time it could have been those of Troeltsch or Max Weber); this emphasis contrasts with interest in an individual author and his stylistic concern.

So the question is that of the community as the place of the tradition; the needs of this community in its worship, its mission, its teaching. For theology, form criticism provided the possibility of no longer grounding Christianity in the historical Jesus but in the proclamation ('the ke-rygma') and the confession of those who acknowledge Jesus as the present Lord after Easter. Now, too, an earlier article by the systematic theologian Martin Kähler was taken up (1835-1912).

The So-Called Historical Jesus and the Historic, Biblical Christ (1892), English translation Fortress Press 1964.

This article is the source of the much-quoted sentence: 'Somewhat provocatively, one could call the Gospels passion narratives with an extended introduction' (60n). The contrast with historical theology becomes clear in the following antithesis: 'I deny that it is the purpose of the Gospels to serve as documentary sources for a scientifically produced biography of Jesus. They did not have such a purpose themselves, nor may church or theology force this purpose on them as being essential to them. Their purpose is to arouse faith in Jesus through vivid proclamation of his activity as saviour' (104). Certainly form-critical questions are in themselves neutral in respect of the historical Jesus in so far as they do not offer any argument for or against the originality of a tradition – moreover Dibelius, like Bultmann, wrote a book about Jesus – but they do draw attention to the purpose of the tradition in the context of the community. So Dibelius attributes all the forms he describes to preaching, with the exception of the crude miracle stories, which he describes as 'Novellen' (70-103, translated in the English text as 'tales'); he cannot recognize any proclamation in them and he attributes them to a later period when early Christianity was already more established in the world. Bultmann makes more marked distinctions when investigating the particular 'setting in life', but for him, too, proclamation is the real motive force in the Jesus tradition.

So what is initially a purely functional (and indeed aesthetic) concern in the questioning thus attains a considerable degree of theological importance and occasionally had to serve as a demonstration (in addition to Schweitzer's book, which was equally misunderstood, see 2.4.2.4) that in any case it is impossible methodologically to arrive at much certain knowledge about the historical Jesus. The interest in the questions was how Christianity is no longer grounded in the historical Jesus but in the proclamation of the saving act of God in this Jesus, in the kerygma, so that kerygmatic theology and form criticism belong closely together in the history of New Testament exegesis.

The kerygmatic character of the tradition cannot be inferred directly from the stories which tell of the past without directly addressing the reader (or hearer); for Dibelius, too, these stories only have their setting in the context of preaching, and are not themselves preaching. Rather, the kerygmatic intent is disclosed from the 'setting in the life' of the community, to which the texts are related through their form. The proclamation on which this community is grounded is not to be found here, but in another sphere of the text.

In his introductory chapter 'Sermons', Dibelius moves via the sermons of the apostles in Acts to I Cor.15.3ff.: 'Alongside of these indirect indications of Acts concerning a primitive-Christian kerygma, there comes a further and significant witness. It is significant above all, in that its testimony points to the earliest period, to St Paul, or rather to the tradition which he hands on in I Cor.15' (18). This text does not simply represent 'the kerygma' – it has other formulations as well – but it is certainly evident here that the kerygma is 'a witness of salvation' (22), i.e. not a detached historical report.

Bultmann, too, refers to these and similar texts in Paul and in Acts and understands the texts of the Gospels as an 'expansion and illustration' of the Christian kerygma; its meaning is: 'The Christ who is proclaimed here is not the historical Jesus but the Christ of faith and the cult. Hence in the foreground of the proclamation of Christ stand the death and resurrection of Jesus Christ as the saving facts which are confessed in faith and become effective for believers in baptism and the Lord's supper' (370).

'Which all amounts to this: the tradition had to be presented as a unity from the point of view that in it he who spoke and was spoken of was he who had lived on earth as son of God, had suffered, died, risen and been exalted to heavenly glory. And inevitably the centre of gravity had to be the end of the story, the passion and resurrection' (371). In the note which goes with this passage Bultmann refers to Kähler's description of the Gospels, quoted above, as 'passion narratives with extended introductions', to A.Schlatter (*Der Glaube im Neuen Testament*, ⁵1963, 477: 'For each of the evangelist the gospel was the story of Jesus' way to the cross'), and to the Catholic theologian, Romano Guardini, *The Spirit of the Liturgy*, 'where the individual stories in the Gospels are understood from their context in the mass' (371 n.2); moreover, this combination gives a clear indication of the new theological orientation on authors who are not from the circles of historical theology.

In the sentences I have quoted Bultmann is in fact describing the way in which he sees the evangelist Mark working : not as a theologian with his own concern to shape the material (see 3.2.2) but as the final point of oral tradition from which the motive force of that tradition can be seen.

From this beginning, form-critical questions were asked about kerygmatic formulae; these emerge from the letters of Paul rather than from the Gospels. Here the starting point was the fact that in I Cor.15.3ff. and also in I Cor.11.23-25 Paul hands on texts which he says he has not formulated himself, but has taken over from the tradition (see 2.2.5). In I Cor.15 he reminds his readers of the origin and foundation of their faith; this text does not speak of the death, burial, resurrection and appearances of Christ as mere 'facts' but describes them in theological terms as being 'in accordance with the scriptures' and having taken place 'for our sins', with saving significance for believers.

In his *Theology of the New Testament* (see 3.1.2.3) Bultmann discussed all the christological statements of the letters of Paul under 'The Kerygma of the Earliest Church' and above all under 'The Kerygma of the Hellenistic Church aside from Paul', not in the Pauline part of the book. This suggested that such texts were not formulated in this way for the first time by Paul, but had come into being in the community. Ernst Käsemann developed something like a methodology of this investigation in a brief article on Romans 3.25; the approach was made more systematic by Hans Conzelmann, who distinguished between 'homology' (the confession 'Jesus is Lord') and 'creed' (the formula of faith: 'God has raised him from the dead') in Rom.10.9.

E.Käsemann, 'Zum Verständnis von Röm.3.24-26', ZNW 43, 1950/51, 150-4, reprinted in Exegetische Versuche und Besinnungen I, Göttingen 1960, 96-100 (this volume also contains further investigations with a similar methodology, e.g. on Phil.2.5-11. Unfortunately the English translation of Käsemann's book, Essays on New Testament Themes, London 1964, is only partial and does not include either of these articles).
H.Conzelmann. 'Was glaubte die frühe Christenheit?', in Theologie als Schrift-auslegung, Beihefte zur Evangelischen Theologie 65, 1974, 106-19.
The question of the kerygma was taken up in Britain in particular by C.H.Dodd, The Apostolic Tradition and its Developments, Hodder and Stoughton 1936, but against a rather different theological background.

The approach here is primarily literary-critical (see 2.2.5), in that such christological texts are isolated as tradition which Paul himself says that he has taken over (I Cor.15.1f.) or, where there is no explicit statement, on the basis of a terminology which is not typical of Paul. The main formal elements are the parallel construction of statements about death and resurrection in sentences of roughly equal length: either baptism ('baptismal confession') or the eucharist (I Cor.11.23-25 and 10.16, and according to Käsemann also Rom.3.25) are assumed as the setting in life.

Here one could refer back to earlier works, above all A.Seeberg, Der Katechismus der Urchristentum, 1903 (reprinted as Theologische Versuche 26, 1966), which attempted to reconstruct something like a complete dogmatics of early Christianity from the writings of the New Testament. In the new theological complex of the quest for the kerygma and in conjunction with history-of-religions questions (the derivation of the formulae from the Palestinian or Hellenistic communities), a new branch of research came into being.

Major studies in this area are:
F.Hahn, Christologische Hoheitstitel, FRLANT 83 [4]1974 (the partial English translation is so flawed as to be not really usable);
W.Kramer, Christ, Lord, Son of God, SBT 50, SCM Press 1966;
K.Wengst, Christologische Formeln und Lieder des Urchristentums, StNT 7, [2]1973.
The themes of O.Cullmann, The Christology of the New Testament, SCM Press and Westminster Press 1959, are similar; however, it does not investigate the relationship between kerygma and theology but systematizes christology in terms of salvation history: the earthly activity of Jesus, his future activity, his present activity.

The most comprehensive survey of this whole area in English is J.D.G.Dunn, *Christology in the Making*, SCM Press and Fortress Press ²1989.

Finally, form-critical work opposed historical theology at yet another point. If Christianity was no longer grounded in the historical Jesus but in the kerygma, at the same time the essential content of Christianity was no longer defined as ethics but as proclamation. In the sphere of New Testament ethics (paraenesis), Dibelius in particular had drawn attention by his combination of form-critical and history-of-religions questions to the fact that the form and content of early Christianity is not original but is dependent above all on traditions of Hellenistic Judaism, where the Old Testament tradition had been mixed with elements from Greek philosophical ethics. At the same time he understood New Testament ethics as being later in time, and as having really originated only out of the need to come to terms with the world when the hope of an imminent end to this world had been shattered.

Cf. M.Dibelius, *Geschichte der urchristlichen Literatur*, 1926, reprinted Theologische Bücherei 58, 1975, 24, and the introduction to his commentary *Der Brief des Jakobus*, Kritisch-exegetischer Kommentar 15, 1921.

3.2.4   Form criticism as exegetical questioning

The defining question for form criticism is:
   What is the form of the text? What purpose does this form have?
   The auxiliary questions are:
   Are there similar texts in the New Testament itself, in the Old Testament, or elsewhere in literature contemporary to early Christianity which have the same form?
   Is it possible to infer a purpose for the text from its form and content?
   In what sphere of the life of the community (worship, teaching, mission, etc.) can the text be placed?
   Form criticism, too, is as strongly formalized in this defining question as the other complexes of exegetical questions. Again the question of truth, which classic form criticism saw in the kerygma and thus behind the texts, is neutralized. At the same time, the replacement of the term 'setting in life' with 'purpose' extends the form-critical question, for example to the letter form as such. The letter does not in fact have a special setting in the life of the community (in the same way as does e.g. a 'Pastoral Letter'), but is a general form of communication between an author and one or more recipients, regardless of whether its subject-matter is commercial, personal, religious or whatever. At the same time this approach abandons any strict differentiation between oral and

written tradition, as both follow definite forms. On the other hand, form criticism should not be carried on as a merely formal classification of texts; the question is always that of 'purpose', the purpose of the form and not of the specific text. (It is always helpful to ask where and for what purpose corresponding forms are used today.)

There is a lack of unity in the literature in the use of 'form' and 'genre' (German *Gattung*). Sometimes the two terms are used as synonyms, sometimes the term 'genre' is limited to literary as opposed to non-literary forms: sometimes 'genre' is used as a more comprehensive term (the gospel is a genre, the dispute is a form within the genre of gospel).

As I have said, the books of Dibelius and Bultmann are still standard works on the form criticism of the synoptic Gospels.

Here the important forms are:

- Apohthegm (plural apothegms or apothegmata), a form from classical literature. This is a short scene which ends in a general statement which transcends the specific occasion (the Greek word itself means simply 'statement, sentence'); all the weight lies on this sentence. Bultmann makes a distinction here, depending on the particular content, between disputes in which there is a conflict over alternative views (e.g. Mark 2.18-22) and scholastic dialogues, in which Jesus gives an answer to a non-polemical question as the teacher of the disciples or of others (e.g. Mark 10.17-31). The 'setting in life' of the apophthegms is the discussion of rules which apply in the community, that of the disputes in controversy with Judaism, and that of the scholastic dialogues in arguments within the community. In Dibelius the corresponding texts appear along with some miracle stories as paradigms, i.e. as examples used in preaching.

- The sayings of Jesus are expressed in a variety of forms, e.g. as rules ('whoever... he') which have a definitive character (cf. Mark 4.22), and as beatitudes ('blessed is he who...') which are also definitive formulations (cf. Luke 6.20-23). There is to some extent a negative parallel in the 'woes': 'Woe to those who...' (cf. Matt.23.13-31). One characteristic of the Jesus tradition in the synoptics is, of course, the parable. Here Bultmann, like Jülicher, makes a distinction between the similitude (German *Gleichnis*) as the description of a regular happening (cf. Mark 4.26-29) and the parable (in German the word is virtually the same, a rendering of Greek *parabole*) as the description of an interesting case which is possible, but does not usually occur (cf. Luke 18.8); in addition he uses 'exemplary narrative' (only in connection with the Gospel of Luke, e.g. 10.30-37, the Good Samaritan). In Dibelius the parables appear as paraenesis: so here too Dibelius investigates the function of the form in the preaching of the community, regardless of how the parables may originally have been meant.

- The miracle stories are the most characteristic narratives. Here

Bultmann makes a distinction in terms of content between healing miracles and nature miracles, whereas Dibelius describes the pure miracle stories as Novellen (see 3.2.3). Stories without the direct character of proclamation are by contrast understood as paradigms. The distinction in terms of content and form arrived at by Gerd Theissen, between exorcisms (driving out of demons), healings, epiphanies (in which the divinity of Jesus is manifest), rescue miracles (rescue from distress at sea), gift miracles (feeding stories) and rule miracles related to norms (sabbath stories), in which a miracle of Jesus is clinching evidence in a conflict, takes things further here.

Gerd Theissen, *Miracle Stories of the Early Christian Tradition*, Edinburgh 1983, 85-112.

Bultmann and Dibelius include under the term 'legend' those stories which have an essentially edifying character; in some there is a portrait of Jesus himself, as in the story of the twelve-year-old Jesus in the temple (Luke 2.41-52), while others describe the origin of a particular custom, as in the accounts of the institution of the eucharist. Here the term 'legend' is free from the negative connotations which it has gained since historicism ('only a legend' – historical research destroys legends) and denotes a particular mode of narration without any historical value-judgment.
- Finally, the passion narratives, which both Dibelius and Bultmann regard as being close to legend understood in the above sense, have a separate chapter in Dibelius, since this is the only material defined by content and not by function. Only here is there a longer narrative complex in which the individual scenes mostly make no sense by themselves, but are related to one another (cf. Mark 14.27-31). The passion story is told not merely out of biographical interest but as proclamation (see 3.2.3).
  None of these forms is as it were 'Christian in origin', but all appear contemporaneously in Jewish and Greek literature: all point to primarily oral forms of the tradition, not a primarily written version. It is important to identify not only 'pure' forms but also mixed forms (Mark 3.1-5 is both miracle story and apophthegm) and overlapping forms (Mark 4.1-34 is a sermon by Jesus which includes both similitudes and rules as well as interpretation of similitudes).
  Nor is the purpose of the forms in each case specifically Christian, though in this tradition it is clear that Jesus is not just a random means of conveying universal truths but rather this truth remains bound to Jesus even where something like a universal truth-claim arises out of a single event (above all in the apophthegms).
  There is some dispute as to how far the overarching form 'gospel' is

a new development and how far forms like ancient biography need to be taken account of here. Compared with the latter, the special feature of the Gospels is certainly their relationship to the community and thus their function in the context of proclamation. But if we generalize this reference to the relationship between author and readers in the sense that every author – whether consciously or not – wants to report something to his readers which transcends what he tells them, then the special feature of the Gospels is their particular content, not their character as proclamation.

Strikingly, there are no disputes in the logia source. Sayings and similitudes predominate; there are, however, also two miracle stories (Matt.8.5-13/Luke 7.1-10; Matt.12.22f./Luke 11.13) and short scenes in the style of apophthegms. The form of the logia source as a whole recalls collections of sayings in the Jewish and Greek tradition. The Gospel of Thomas (see 2.3.3) also belongs in this tradition; here individual sayings stereotyped by 'Jesus said' are collected together; they are only rarely extended to short scenes.

In the Gospel of John, the only forms which are known to us from the synoptic Gospels are the miracle stories and the passion narrative. The long discourses elude any definition in terms of form criticism, since apart from the 'I am' sayings they really do not display any formal characteristics.

There are miracle stories in Acts, the form of which corresponds to those in the Gospels. However, the speeches by the apostles, in which we hear primarily the voice of the author who in the style of the ancient historian gives his commentary on events in them, do also follow forms of primitive Christian proclamation.

M.Dibelius, 'The Speeches in Acts and Ancient Historiography', in *Studies in the Acts of the Apostles*, SCM Press and Scribners 1956, 138-191;
U.Wilckens, *Die Missionsreden der Apostelgeschichte*, WMANT 5, [2]1963;
D.L.Aune, *The New Testament in its Literary Environment*, Westminster Press 1987 and James Clarke 1988.

In the letters, the term 'letter' itself already denotes a form which as such is primarily independent of a particular author's concern for form and style. The distinction proposed by A. Deissmann (see 2.3.3) between real letters, which are related to a specific situation, and 'epistles' as treatises in the form of letters without any real reference to a situation, is the basis for a first rough distinction, though one must not associate any value judgments with it.

W.G.Doty, *Letters in Primitive Christianity*, Fortress Press 1973.

The letters of Paul all begin with a 'prescript' in which the sender(s) is/

are mentioned in the nominative and the recipients in the dative (cf. I Cor.1.1f.). A new sentence follows, which always begins with 'Grace and peace – to you' (cf. I Cor.1.3). This takes up the usual introduction to Greek letters which appears in the New Testament in Acts 15.23; 23.26; James 1.1, but varies it by replacing the greeting *chairein* with a formula of blessing introduced by the cognate noun *charis*.

Then follows the *proemium*, the introduction to the letter proper, which expresses the relationship between author and recipients, just as we might begin a letter by saying thank-you. Here a thanksgiving is made to God, introduced with 'I/we thank' (cf. I Cor.1-3-9) or (thus II Cor.1.3; cf.Eph.1.3) 'Praise be to God'; here the thanks to God is directly transformed into a prayer of thanksgiving. The reason why such thanksgiving is – exceptionally – absent in Gal.1.6 is because of the particular situation in Galatia – here there is nothing to say thank you for, since sender and recipients are completely at odds.

The main part of the letter proper is less governed by form: here the forms depend on the particular situation, the degree of information which Paul has and also the way in which he has been informed. In I Cor.7.1 Paul refers to a question from the Corinthians which has been sent to him in writing; elsewhere he has evidently been informed by word of mouth (cf. I Cor.1.1).

Towards the end of the letters sections regularly appear which begin 'I/we admonish' (cf. I Cor.16.15) – again Galatians is an exception. These sections are of varying length, in Romans e.g. one begins at 12.1. Then there are usually special greetings from and/or to particular people, and a formula of blessing rounds the letter off (in I Cor.16.20-24 it is perhaps woven into elements of a liturgy).

In addition to the beginnings already made, the question has to be asked how far this letter-form itself and the forms occurring in it are to be seen in the context of rhetorical forms and similar literary forms from antiquity. For a long time it has been recognized that Paul takes over motives and figures of speech from the 'diatribe', the popular philosophical instruction of his time: rhetorical questions, fictitious objections, entreaties and so on. Also relevant in this context is the fact that in I Cor.9.3 Paul explicitly describes the remarks which follow as an apology (a speech in his defence) and then turns to his judges like an accused person in court, seeking in rhetorical questions to persuade them to agree to his view. Questions of form and purpose are also important in sections from the letters, not just the question of a particular situation, and the picture that we have of the specific situation can shift if we see that a question which Paul takes up need not necessarily have been put to him by others, but follows from the argument that he himself is pursuing.

When examining the passages taken by Paul from the tradition (see 2.2.5) we have to raise the form-critical question independently of the context in which the passages appear in Paul. However, it is questionable here whether the confessional formulae are to be put in the setting of baptism. Against this is the fact that there is no evidence of real baptismal confessions until very much later. These 'confessions' are to be understood more as brief summaries of faith, the wording of which can vary considerably. There are types of passage in paraenesis which constantly recur, like the 'catalogues of virtues and vices', but similarly these too do not have a stereotyped wording.

In the case of both the summaries of faith and paraenesis we may expect that particular themes which are varied in oral preaching will have found a form, even if this was open. However, it is worth reflecting that despite all the intensive work on such pre-Pauline traditions, our picture of early Christian worship is still pale – and judging by I Cor.12-14 such liturgies will have been very different from the sermon, baptism, eucharist and instruction that we know from Protestant liturgy.

Since evidently only letters of Paul (no sermons, prayers or whatever) were available when people began to safeguard his legacy, the letter became a special form of theological presentation and argument. The writings composed under his name and now usually regarded as being inauthentic (Colossians, Ephesians, II Thessalonians and the Pastorals) adopted this form, and other writings in the canon are also regarded as letters, even if they contain few if any elements of a letter, as in the case of I John and Hebrews. By means of real or more or less stylized problems (it is sometimes hard to tell which is which in individual instances), these documents present a theological position, and this approach extends beyond the realm of the New Testament to the letters which are included among the 'Apostolic Fathers' (see 1.1.5).

From the form-critical perspective the Letter of James is particularly interesting; in his commentary (see 3.2.3) Dibelius gave it the form and function of paraenesis, though one must differ from his view that there is no theology in James.

Finally, in the Revelation of John it is possible to draw some conclusions from the scattered hymns (see 2.2.5) to the hymns of the community. Revelation, too, begins in 1.4-3.22 with seven letters to various communities. The pattern of vision and interpretation which then governs the book proper corresponds in function to apocalypses in the Jewish tradition.

In the course of the second century, more demanding forms then emerged alongside those of the gospel and the letter, which still continued to be fostered: the apology (as a writing in defence of Christianity to the emperor), the dialogue, the tractate (as a connected thematic discussion) and already commentaries on Gospels, and also poetic forms. This certainly allows us to conclude that the level of education was rising within the Christian communities. However, the writings from the beginnings of Christianity were not replaced by new ones; rather, this was the time when the collection was begun which then became the canon (see 1.1.2).

3.3   The question of the theology of the evangelists: redaction criticism

3.3.1   The basic problem

The basic problem of redaction criticism arises from the fact that in the four Gospels we have very different accounts of who Jesus was, what he said and did. Literary criticism (see 2.2.4) went behind the Gospels in search of reliable sources from which the real Jesus was to be depicted; form criticism investigated the tradition taken up by the evangelists and its setting in the life of the community (see 3.2.3). With redaction criticism, interest turned to the Gospels as we have them and thus to the particular profile of individual evangelists who sought, each in his own way, with the help of the tradition at his disposal, to communicate theological truth in the light of his contemporary sitation.

3.3.2   Beginnings in form criticism and literary criticism

The term 'redaction criticism' was used for the first time by Willi Marxsen (*Mark the Evangelist*, Abingdon Press 1969, 21), by analogy with 'form criticism'. It is thus associated with the terminology of form criticism, which saw the evangelists as collectors and perhaps 'redactors' of the tradition. In other words they were writers who merely collected existing material and added a few emphases of their own. However, redaction criticism means more, since it raises the question of the theological conceptions of the individual evangelists.

Form criticism was to some degree opposed to literary criticism, but redaction criticism was again drawn back more strongly to literary criticism: if one is investigating the redaction of material, one must first ask what the material on which the redactor worked looked like. To achieve a theological profile of, say, the Gospel of Matthew it is necessary to presuppose the two-source theory (see 2.2.4) and compare Matthew with Mark as one of the sources that he uses.

Both Bultmann and Dibelius described the redactional work of the evangelists in their books on form criticism (see 3.2.2), though predominantly from a stylistic perspective. Bultmann described the Gospel of Mark as 'the union of the Hellenistic kerygma about Christ... with the tradition of the story of Jesus' (347f.). In so doing he referred, *inter alia*, to W.Wrede (*The Messianic Secret in the Gospels* (1901, English translation James Clarke 1971), who had attributed the passages in the Gospels in which Jesus is spoken of as the Messiah or the Son of God (e.g. Mark 8.27ff.; 14.61f.) to the 'dogmatics' of the community and not to the self-awareness of the historical Jesus. And Bultmann takes over the characterization of the Gospel of Mark as a 'book of secret epiphanies' from Dibelius (*From Tradition to Gospel*, 230).

Thus the presupposition of the Gospel of Mark is the 'kerygma', that 'in all the sayings of Jesus which were reported, he speaks who is recognized in faith and worship as Messiah or Lord, and who, as the proclamation makes known his works and hands on his sayings, is actually present for the church' (348). However, in this way the Gospel of Mark is merely the end-point of the tradition, since that is also true of the tradition itself (see 3.2.3): the evangelist is only the collector and redactor, and has no distinctive profile which marks him off from the tradition.

Accordingly Dibelius discusses the Gospel of Mark in his chapter on 'Collecting' (*Sammlung*, misleading rendered 'Synthesis' in the English translation). He too describes the process of collection essentially in terms of form and style and similarly refers to Wrede. The purpose of Mark is: 'To represent Jesus as the Messiah, but without placing his work in a supernatural sphere which had no room for tradition – although this was done in the Fourth Gospel. It is also to emphasize those characteristics in the tradition which disclose Jesus as Messiah, but at the same time to show why he was not recognized as Messiah by the people and why he was opposed, despised and finally sent to the cross. In this way the Gospel of Mark was written as a book of secret epiphanies. Both the parables and the tales (Novellen) can be brought under this heading' (232). Dibelius' view of the conception underlying the Gospel is thus very similar to Bultmann's perspective on christology.

In discussing the Gospel of Matthew Bultmann primarily stresses the basic agreement with Mark. The real reason why Matthew nevertheless makes a different impression from Mark is that he arranges the material differently ('to give his gospel the strongest impression of a catechism or teaching book', 356). Bultmann sees Matthew's distinctive emphases – here following Schlatter and others – in a stronger connection with the church, in the heightening of the figure of Jesus so that it becomes divine, and in the theme of the fulfilment of Old Testament prophecy.

In Dibelius, by contrast, there is no summary account of either Matthew or Luke.

For Luke, too, Bultmann stresses the continuity with Mark despite the not inconsiderable transpositions of material. He sees the main interest of the evangelist Luke as being in the literary rather than the theological sphere: 'the Gospel of Luke is the climax of the history of the synoptic tradition in so far as the development which the tradition had undergone from the beginning has attained its greatest success in Luke: the editing and connecting of isolated sections into a coherent continuity' (367).

Bultmann also speaks of 'collection and redaction' in this sense in connection with the logia source Q (329-37). However, he avoids the term 'theology' for both Q and the synoptic Gospels as a whole, not least because he understands 'theology' to be a conceptual explanation of faith (see 3.1.2.3) which cannot be found in the synoptic Gospels – in contrast to the Gospel of John. They refer only to the kerygma, the proclamation of Jesus as the present Lord, and do not develop this in connection with the position of human beings before God.

3.3.3   The questions raised by redaction criticism

A short article by Günther Bornkamm, 'The Stilling of the Storm in the Gospel of Matthew', is identified as the beginning of the questions raised by redaction criticism proper, though here Bornkamm quite emphatically begins with form criticism. But he shows by means of Matt.8.23-27 that Matthew is 'not only a hander-on of the narrative but also its oldest exegete' (55), and ends after a warning against over-interpretation with a pointer which he and others subsequently follow: 'This makes all the more important the proof of definite theological intentions' (57).

G.Bornkamm, 'The Stilling of the Storm in Matthew', in G.Bornkamm, G.Barth and H.J.Held, *Tradition and Interpretation in Matthew*, SCM Press ²1982.

So here theology proves to be the exegesis of already existing tradition, and this is given programmatic expression in the title of the book mentioned above; the interpretation is related to a particular situation. With this second aspect, the relationship to a situation, fruitful use is made of a phrase of Julius Schniewind's, who had described the gospels as 'kerygma of a definite situation and task' (*Tradition and Interpretation*, 12). This approach is carried through by Held on the miracle stories and by Bornkamm on the discourses and is applied by

Barth to the understanding of the law in Matthew. Common to all three is the thesis that Matthew was engaged on two fronts: he had to distinguish himself on the one hand from the Jewish tradition which was being refounded after the destruction of Jerusalem (the 'better' righteousness, cf. 5.20), and on the other also from trends in early Christianity in which the view was that with Jesus the law had been abrogated (the 'antinomians' – cf. 5.17). The real achievement of the evangelist is his interpretation of the tradition which had come down to him in the face of these two fronts under the headings of law and righteousness, church, christology and discipleship.

Hans Conzelmann was the first to raise redaction-critical questions about the Gospel of Luke and its continuation in Acts in his book *Die Mitte der Zeit. Studien zur Theologie des Lukas* (1977: the English title, *The Theology of St Luke*, London 1960, reissued 1982, unfortunately omits the important first half of the German title, 'The Middle of Time'; this indicates the focal point of Conzelmann's approach, see below). He too begins from form criticism, but notes how in Luke kerygma and history diverge: 'Whereas in Mark the narrative itself provides a broad unfolding of the kerygma, Luke defines the narrative as the historical foundation, which is added as a secondary factor to the kerygma, a knowledge of which he takes for granted' (11). The German title of the book indicates the main thesis: the 'middle of time' is the time of Jesus, which is preceded by the time of Israel and followed by the time of the church. The reason for this conception is that: 'Luke is confronted by the situation in which the church finds herself by the delay of the Parousia and her existence in secular history, and he tries to come to terms with the situation by his account of historical events' (14). So – after a section on Luke's ideas of geography – Conzelmann's method is to investigate the effect of this conception on the great dogmatic themes of eschatology, salvation history, christology and the church. Thus in Luke theology proves to be a conscious reflection on these themes. However, for all Conzelmann's understanding of the historical situation of Luke this outline remains problematical, although he does not rate Luke in such a negative way as others or dismiss him as 'early Catholic', which in the Protestant context means the beginning of the decline from a good start.

While further discussion led to criticism of details of Conzelmann's arguments, it was in fact dominated by the question whether the way in which Luke does theology as a historian is legitimate or not. Dibelius had already answered in the affirmative in his article 'The First Christian Historian', which was written with much sympathy for Luke: 'Thus, through the literary methods of the historian, he was able to discharge his other obligation of being a preacher of faith in Christ.'

M.Dibelius, 'The First Christian Historian', in *Studies in the Acts of the Apostles*, SCM Press and Scribners 1956, 123-37 (the quotation is the last sentence of the article).

The redaction-critical interpretation of the Gospel of Mark begins with Marxsen's 1956 book *Mark the Evangelist*, which has already been mentioned. He too begins with form criticism, but does not regard redaction criticism as a direct continuation of form criticism (as do Bornkamm and Conzelmann): 'Theoretically it would have been possible for redaction-critical research to have begun immediately after literary criticism' (21), since literary criticism was concerned to work out the tradition by leaving aside the redaction, and redaction criticism was now doing things the other way round. However, the proximity to form criticism emerges in the relationship between the text and the community, i.e. in the sociological element of form criticism: 'But over against form criticism this element is joined to an "individualistic" trait oriented to the particular interest and point of view of the evangelist concerned' (24).

Marxsen then tries to work out Mark's particular conception on the basis of four themes: the description of John the Baptist, the geographical outline and above all the role of Galilee in it; the concept of *euaggelion*, which he interprets as having been inserted by Mark redactionally in all the passages in which it occurs, and finally eschatology, characterized as an ardent expectation of an imminent end on the basis of Mark 13.

Like Bornkamm, Marxsen works by investigating the relation between tradition and redaction. Marxsen himself points out how problematical this is, since it involves a circular argument. In contrast to Matthew and Luke, here the tradition first has to be reconstructed. Marxsen keeps to Bultmann's view of the evangelist, namely that Mark 'ties together... the Pauline kerygma and the (so-called) synoptic tradition' (216). However, his emphasis is new in that he thinks that in this way Mark was countering a gnosticizing of Paul's message, i.e. a theology which detached the saving event completely from the earthly Jesus.

The most problematical feature is Marxsen's attempt to relate the Gospel to the specific situation of the community for which Mark is writing, and indeed he later abandoned the thesis which he put forward at that time, namely that the Gospel of Mark as a whole is a call to await the parousia, when Jesus will return, in Galilee, a call which was connected historically with the final phase of the Jewish War in 66-70 CE.

In subsequent developments in redaction criticism, first of all a series of further investigations appeared on the Gospel of Matthew.

There is a convenient survey of the contents of these books, which have not been translated, in Joachim Rohde, *Rediscovering the Teaching of the Evangelists*, SCM Press and Westminster Press 1969. Matthew is covered on pp. 47-112.
W.Trilling, *Das wahre Israel*, StANT 10, 1959, [3]1964;
G.Strecker, *Der Weg der Gerechtigkeit*, FRLANT 82, 1962;
R.Hummel, *Die Auseinandersetzung zwischen Kirche und Judentum im Matthäus evangelium*, Beihefte zur Evangelischen Theologie 33, 1963;
R.Walker, *Die Heilsgeschichte im ersten Evangelium*, FRLANT 91, 1967;
H.Frankemölle, *Jahwebund und Kirche Christi*, 1974;
E.Schweizer, *Good News according to Matthew*, John Knox Press and SPCK 1976, is also orientated on redaction criticism.

The main point of dispute is whether the Gospel of Matthew is to be described as Jewish Christian (thus Bornkamm and Barth) or Gentile Christian (thus Trilling and Strecker). Here the basic problem of redaction criticism emerges: questions are asked about the theology of the evangelist and the situation of his readers, but all that is known of the evangelist is a name which may well be only putative, and we have no information about any geographical or historical situation; for both these the only source is inferences from the work itself.

Here the alternatives named are not arbitrary. Either Matthew comes from the Jewish tradition which he now understands anew in terms of the Christian kerygma – that is what is meant by 'Jewish Christian' – or from the start he is engaged in a polemical argument with the Jewish tradition from the Christian standpoint – as a 'Gentile Christian'. The understanding of the law and thus the theme of righteousness in the Gospel will be interpreted differently, depending on the alternative chosen.

The redaction-critical interpretation of the Gospel of Luke has not been developed so much in books as in articles, first of all discussing the question already mentioned, as to how the theology of Luke, designated by the term 'salvation history', is to be evaluated in theological terms.

See Joachim Rohde, *Rediscovering the Teaching of the Evangelists*, 153-239;
W.C.Robinson, *Der Weg des Herrn*, Theologische Forschung 36, 1964;
Helmut Flender, *St Luke. Theologian of Redemptive History*, SPCK 1967;
M.Dömer, *Das Heil Gottes*, Bonner Biblische Beiträge 51, 1978; E.Schweizer, *Good News according to Luke*, John Knox Press and SPCK 1984, has a redaction-critical emphasis.

So much redaction-critical work has been done on the Gospel of

Mark that it is almost impossible to survey. Though there was some initial delay, this is the work which attracted the greatest interest.

See Joachim Rohde, *Rediscovering the Teaching of the Evangelists*, 113-52.

Here the problem focusses above all on the question of the relationship between tradition and redaction, on which there is no kind of consensus nor even a reduction to a few basic possibilities. The spectrum ranges from the view that Mark only takes up his tradition, especially the miracle stories, to refute it, to a complete identification of tradition and redaction. Accordingly, both the evangelist's conception and the situation of his readers are defined in very different ways.

Several new commentaries tend towards redaction criticism:
E.Schweitzer, *Good News according to Mark*, John Knox Press and SPCK 1971;
J.Gnilka, *Das Evangelium nach Markus*, two vols, Evangelisch-Katholischer Kommentar 2, 1978/79;
R.Pesch, *Das Markusevangelium*, two vols, Herders Theologischer Kommentar 2, 1976/77;
W.Schmithals, *Das Evangelium nach Markus*, two vols, Ökumenischer Taschenbuch-Kommentar 2, 1979.
Each of the two last solves the problem of the relationship between tradition and redaction in his own way: Pesch identifies redaction and tradition almost completely; Schmithals reconstructs a 'basic document' behind the Gospel of Mark as we now have it and makes it the real text to be interpreted.

Given this confused situation in the case of the Gospel of Mark, it is surprising that answers to the question of the redaction of the Logia source are much more in accord. Here the possible solutions are reduced to the alternatives that Q was composed either in two successive stages (thus Schulz and Polag), or as a single redaction of a variety of traditions (thus Hoffmann and Lührmann).

D.Lührmann, *Die Redaktion der Logienquelle*, WMANT 33, 1969;
P.Hoffmann, *Studien zur Theologie der Logienquelle*, NTA Neue Folge 8, 1972;
S.Schulz, *Die Spruchquelle der Evangelisten*, 1972;
R.A.Edwards, *A Theology of Q*, Fortress Press 1976; A.P.Polag, *Die Christologie der Logienquelle*, WMANT 45, 1977.

In contrast to form criticism, which related Q to the kerygma and took this as a background of interpretation (see 3.2.3), an attempt is made in redaction-critical interpretation of the logia source to derive a christology from this tradition itself which is not orientated on the passion kerygma but is based on a conception of the continuation of the activity of Jesus in the action of the disciples.

3.3.4   Redaction criticism as exegetical questioning

The defining question of redaction criticism is:

How does the author of a written work incorporate into his text a tradition the wording of which is already given?

Auxiliary questions:

Is it possible to recognize transformations of the tradition that is adopted?

Is it possible to observe an ongoing tendency of the author in dealing with the tradition available to him?

What function does a tradition have in the context of the writing in which it is included?

So redaction criticism has to interact with literary criticism, since like literary criticism it separates tradition from redaction. Thus the possibilities of its work are given beforehand by literary criticism; redaction criticism can be used wherever there are corresponding · literary-critical phenomena (see 2.2.5).

Since this exegetical approach is so recent, there is less formalization in the defining question than in the case of the other questioning, though there is a considerable difference, in that the questioning is no longer about the kerygma of the evangelists; it is now extended to any work on the tradition.

For the synoptic Gospels, the present state of the problems has essentially been described in the account of the origin of redaction criticism (3.3.3). There will perhaps be new possibilities in the interpret-ation of the Gospel of Mark and also the Logia source if an attempt is made to discover their theological conceptions not so much from the redaction of tradition (since its extent and character is uncertain) as from inner connections.

In the case of the Gospel of John there has long been talk of an 'ecclesiastical redaction'. Its extent and theological significance are disputed. Recently, various works by G.Richter have become significant here; Richter sees a three-stage process of tradition behind the Gospel as we have it which reflects the history of the Johannine commmuity.

G.Richter, *Studien zum Johannesevangelium*, ed. J.Hainz, Biblische Untersu-chungen 13, 1977, cf. also the commentary by J.Becker, *Das Evangelium nach Johannes*, two vols, Ökumenischer Taschenbuch-Kommentar 4, 1979/81, which takes up Richter's theses critically.

Redactional criticism on the Acts of the Apostles is difficult on the one hand because in literary-critical terms there are hardly any clear indications of the traditional material which has doubtless been used, and on the other hand it is the second volume of a two-volume work by the same author, the first of which is the Gospel of Luke; and the very fact that the Gospel is continued into church history is significant for redaction criticism.

The conception of theology as exegesis of tradition as been taken up for the letters of Paul above all by Bornkamm, Käsemann and Conzelmann. Since it had been possible by means of literary criticism and form criticism (see 2.2.5 and 3.2.4) to isolate traditions in the letters which go back to community tradition, so now conversely it can be asked how Paul interprets the tradition which he takes up. For christological tradition that means that Paul interprets it (the 'kerygma') in terms of justification by faith alone (as 'theology'). For Conzelmann this becomes a basic statement about the theology of Paul generally: it is 'interpretation of the creed'.

G.Bornkamm, *Paul*, Hodder and Stoughton and Harper and Row 1975; E.Käsemann, 'The Saving Significance of the Death of Jesus in Paul', in id., *Perspectives on Paul*, SCM Press and Fortress Press 1969, 32-59; H.Conzelmann, 'Die Rechtfertigungslehre des Paulus: Theologie oder Anthropologie?', *Evangelische Theologie* 28, 1968, 389-404, reprinted in id., *Theologie als Schriftauslegung*, Beihefte zur Evangelischen Theologie 65, 1974, 91-206.

In redaction criticism, those who are led by literary criticism to see the letters of Paul as being made up of parts of letters which originated in different situations must find some significance in the redactional version of the letters as we now have them. Here Bornkamm's interpretation of II Corinthians from a form-critical perspective is most convincing.

G.Bornkamm, 'Die Vorgeschichte des sogenannten Zweiten Korintherbrief', in *Geschichte und Glaube* II, Beihefte zur Evangelischen Theologie 53, 1971, 162-94.

Though redaction-critical questions with their understanding of theology as an interpretation of tradition for a particular situation have thus proved fruitful, it has led to a multiplicity of theologies in the New Testament. Whereas liberal theology saw the point of unity in the historical Jesus, and form criticism in the kerygma, it now emerges that there are theologies in the New Testament which take the words and actions of the earthly Jesus as normative – not a 'historical' Jesus as historical theology understood him, but the Jesus who is confessed by his community as present Lord. Rather – and this is particularly true of the synoptic Gospels – they relate particularly to what according to their accounts Jesus said either about law and righteousness (the Sermon on the Mount in Matthew) or Jesus himself said about the difference between his own time and the that of the future community (Mark 2.19f.; Luke 22.35f.). This last theme is taken up in particular in the farewell discourses of the Gospel of John.

On the other hand, Paul does not solve problems in his communities by reference to a normative saying or a normative form of behaviour by Jesus, but draws conclusions from the kerygma. Only rarely does he take up sayings of Jesus at all (see 2.2.5), and then he does not make them binding (in I Cor.7.10 his starting point, contrary to a saying of the Lord, is that divorce can happen; and he himself does not observe the commandment in I Cor.9.14).

Thus the various theologies in the New Testament are not simply interpretations of a common starting point conditioned by the situation; they already begin from different starting points. The question that arises from this for theological value-judgments is posed especially by the theology of Luke (see 3.3.3); this is discussed under the heading of 'early Catholicism', 'canon in the canon' or the 'centre of scripture'. Again the question is the authentic and original nature of Christianity – no longer a Jesus reconstructed in historical terms, as in historical theology, but not the kerygma either. And so there are open questions as well as results in theological exegesis.

3.4 Results and open questions in theological exegesis

3.4.1 Exegesis and the ecumenical world

Neither historical-critical exegesis nor theological exegesis have been accepted in the Protestant churches without opposition, because neither has understood itself to be mere 'method' but rather a reconstruction of theological truth after the destruction of church teaching. In all phases the relationship of exegesis to dogmatics has been problematical, from its beginning in Gabler's distinction between the eternal truth of the biblical writings and the time-conditioned form of dogmatic teaching at any period (in the article mentioned in 1.1.5), through Troeltsch's alternative (in the article discussed in 2.4.2.2, the conclusion of which clearly relates to tactics in church politics), to the dispute over Bultmann's programme of demythologizing.

The question has always been how the origins of Christianity are to be described in historical terms, and also that of the authentic and essential nature of Christianity; and such a judgment had to be made not only in an academic context but also in the context of the church. There have been understandings between exegesis and the church, most recently in the endorsement of critical theology in the Confessing Church – however, Bultmann's reminiscences sound almost ironical: 'with my friend Hans von Soden I endeavoured to see that free scholarly work retained its proper place within it in spite of reactionary tendencies.' This understanding can be studied in the lives of exegetes like G.Bornkamm, E.Käsemann, H.Schlier, E.Fuchs, H.Braun and others.

The Bultmann quotation comes from 'Autobiographical Reflections of Rudolf Bultmann', in C.W.Kegley (ed.), *The Theology of Rudolf Bultmann*, SCM Press and Harper and Row 1966, xxi.

Not just an understanding between exegesis and Protestantism but their identity was put forward as a programme by Gerhard Ebeling in his article 'The Significance of the Critical Historical Method for Church and Theology in Protestantism' in 1950.

The article appears in G.Ebeling, *Word and Faith*, SCM Press and Fortress Press 1965, 17-61.

Whereas Troeltsch located the historical-critical method in the Enlightenment rather than in the difference between Protestantism and Catholicism (see 2.4.2.2), Ebeling identifies the historical-critical method with the scriptural principle of the Lutheran tradition. Here the contrast is with Catholicism, which at that time had dashed all hopes of an understanding between confessions with the 1950 dogma of the physical assumption of Mary. Ebeling refers above all to the sphere of the historical-critical method, which has been depicted as 'theological exegesis' and which he describes as a 'radical return to the theology of the Reformers' (18). In view of the development between the Reformation and the present 'the question boils down to this: what is the relationship between the return to the theology of the Reformers which is now demanded and practised and the critical historical method which has meantime attained increasing, and in the second half of the nineteenth century well nigh undisputed, dominance in theology' (18).

Ebeling sees the significance of the Reformation for theology like this: 'Theology becomes primarily exegesis. And historical exegesis at that, which breaks through the accumulated rubble of tradition to the original text. Further – as is already indicated by the last remark – theology becomes critical theology' (36), in distinction from Catholic theology, which is orientated on tradition. If historical-critical exegesis proper is only a product of modern times, Protestant theology has followed this course: 'Indeed, I venture to assert that the Protestantism of the nineteenth century, by deciding in principle for the critical historical method, maintained and confirmed over against Roman Catholicism in a different situation the decision of the Reformers in the sixteenth century' (55). According to Ebeling this corresponds to the Reformation understanding of faith: 'Faith is exposed to all the vulnerability and ambiguity of the historical... And thus we are justified in asking whether a theology which evades the claims of the critical-historical method has still any idea at all of the genuine meaning of the Reformers' doctrine of justification, even when the formulae of the sixteenth century are repeated with the utmost correctness' (56f.).

However, that does not apply to all the errors of historical criticism, but particularly to the 'questions raised by the religious-historical or form-critical methods' (59). Finally: 'critical historical theology' is not identical with liberal theology. It is, however, the indispensable means of reminding the church of the freedom rooted in the *iustificatio impii*' (60).

In this programmatic sketch Ebeling not only claimed, like Bultmann (see 3.1.2.3), that the tasks of exegetical and dogmatic theology had come to coincide, but also argued for the identity of Reformation theology and church through the historical-critical method: it marks out the difference from Catholicism in modern times as a development of the Reformation scripture principle.

Now in fact my account of the history of exegesis in this book has largely been limited to its history in German Protestantism. The discussion has been limited in this way because what is now regarded as 'New Testament exegesis' derives essentially from this tradition, though it can now be done in the context of very different theological traditions. In recent decades this legacy of German Protestantism has been taken over in an amazing way, not only in the English-speaking world or within Catholic theology but also e.g. in the Orthodox Church.

For this last sphere see the journal *Deltion Biblikon Meleton* (Bulletin of Biblical Studies) which has been appearing in the Greek language in Athens since 1971. This process of reception can be seen in more than the translation of German-language articles. As for the Anglo-Saxon world, a large number of books in German (including this one) are translated into English, and this offers the opportunity – to put it cautiously – of at least getting to know the kind of exegesis which is practised in Germany.

The history of exegesis in the Netherlands, in England, in Scotland and Scandinavia, the other great areas of non-Catholic theology, took a different course from that in Germany, despite the common roots in the Enlightenment. The reason for this was first the different context of exegesis in the churches and the academic world, and also the specifically German concern with Hegel and his consequences, which did not have so direct an influence on the development of exegesis into historical theology as they did elsewhere.

Contacts between British, Dutch and German New Testament scholars in connection with the 1937 Faith and Order conferences led to plans being made for international ecumenical collaboration which found expression in the organization of the *Studiorum Novi Testament Societas*. After the Second World War this made it possible for New Testament scholars to meet one another. North America was increasingly drawn in, as finally was Catholic exegesis (the journal of the society is *New Testament Studies*, *NTS*, which also prints reports of the annual meetings).

The most surprising development is the acceptance of exegesis in the Catholic sphere, above all in Germany and Belgium, but now too in Italy and Spain – and here again the United States of America has played a major role. Whereas a pioneer like Friedrich Wilhelm Maier still had painful experiences as a result of his involvement in New Testament criticism, after the *Instructio de historica Evangeliorum veritate* of 1964 and the Second Vatican Council the way was open, for example, for the adoption of the two-source theory or for judgments on the authorship of the books of the New Testmaent. Of course, in the 1943 encyclical *Divino afflante Spiritu* Pius XII had already cautiously opened the way for the use of historical-critical methods, but despite this, Ebeling could still write his article in 1950 (for this encyclical see the long note on pp.52-5). After 1964 his comments were out of date.

Exegesis blossomed tremendously in the sphere of Catholic theology during the following period. H.Zimmermann's *Neutestamentliche Methodenlehre*, first published in 1967, was reprinted in large quantities several times and reached a sixth edition in 1978, the last to be edited by the author himself. It presents the classic repertoire of exegesis: textual criticism, literary criticism, form criticism, redaction criticism (there is no history of religions, but this is also absent from most textbooks or study books). However, there were two significant points:
- first, the 1943 encyclical was interpreted to mean that 'the Catholic exegete is not only allowed, but obliged, to use the historical-critical method' (17 n.1);
- secondly, the relationship of form criticism and redaction criticism to the church was now interpreted quite differently with an appeal to the First Vatican Council as the basis for 'the presupposition that the church existed before the New Testament and that the canon of the New Testament is grounded wholly in the authority of the church' (30).

All in all the question here remains whether historical-critical exegesis is simply taken over as a formal method – Ebeling, Käsemann and Conzelmann had all argued against such a misunderstanding in the face of the English (and also the Catholic) reception of form criticism. On the other hand, the potential of exegesis as criticism of pre-existing dogma is again being fully realized, as is clear from the controversies over Hans Küng and Edward Schillebeeckx, who base their controversial theses primarily on historical criticism.

Be this as it may, exegesis in the sense described in this book can no longer be defined specifically as Protestant exegesis; those who read articles by Protestant or Catholic exegetes are not usually clear from what they are reading whether the exegete is a Catholic or a Protestant, except for example when it comes to the topic of Peter, which because of its connections with the Pope is still viewed differently in the different confessions.

However, the phenomenon as such is quite ambivalent:

– Is not exegesis in each case done in a very different theological (and academic) context?
– Can exegesis be so formalized that it can be carried on in any context?
– Is exegesis then only a neutral method which can legitimate and/or criticize any kind of theology?
– Does such formalization of exegesis represent a loss of identity in Protestantism so that it is now defined merely as a traditional version of Christianity, particularly in the way in which it deals with scripture?
– Must not the ecumenical world always have an international character, beyond the limits of language and particular backgrounds in the history of theology?
– Can exegesis developed in a specifically German historical context be a model for dealing with biblical texts in quite different contexts? And vice versa, can German theological exegesis learn from exegesis which asks theological questions in other contexts?

3.4.2   The historical Jesus and the kerygma

The attempt of historical theology to find legitimation in the historical Jesus had failed (see 2.4). Theological exegesis had radicalized this insight and seen the kerygma, not the historical Jesus, as the origin of Christianity and theology (3.1). The exegetical questioning which corresponded to this approach was form criticism, which by inquiring into the setting in life came upon the community as the vehicle of the Jesus tradition (see 3.2).

The new quest of the historical Jesus in the 1950s did not go back to historical theology, but began from the observation of the redaction critics that the evangelists throughout do not show interest just in the kerygma but also in Jesus – not the 'historical' Jesus in the modern sense, but the pre-Easter, earthly Jesus (see 3.3). The starting point for this discussion was an article by Ernst Käsemann, 'The Problem of the Historical Jesus', written in 1954.

This article is contained in E.Käsemann, *Essays on New Testament Themes*, SCM Press 1964, 15-47.

After looking back on the controversies between dialectical and liberal theology and on form criticism, Käsemann describes the situation like this: 'the classic liberal question about the Jesus of history is increasingly regaining its theological importance; and, paradoxically, this is happening at a time when liberalism is discredited over wide areas of church life, and happening as a counter-blast to an historical and theological criticism which itself sprang from the soil of liberalism' (17). The way to the historical Jesus does not by-pass the kerygma, but must always take into account the fact that earliest Christianity did not write the Gospels 'primarily as reportage', so that 'its own kerygma actually overlays and conceals the figure of the historical Jesus, thus facing us as historians with incalculable difficulties and very often making any reconstruction quite impossible' (19f.). However, 'to state the paradox as sharply as possible: the community takes so much trouble to maintain historical continuity with him who once trod this earth that it allows the historical events of this earthly life to pass for the most part into oblivion and replaces them by its own message' (20), a process which repeats itself throughout church history.

The real problem is caused by the Gospels, which 'present the earthly tidings of the Christ within the framework of the story of the earthly life of Jesus' (21). Since in the Gospel of John 'the merely historical only has interest and value to the extent to which it mirrors symbolically the recurring experience of Christian faith' and in the Gospel of Mark the story of Jesus is 'mythicized', 'when we inquire where in our Gospels a stronger emphasis is laid on the historical element, we are really left only with Matthew and Luke' (22). So here Käsemann takes up the redaction-critical question and now raises it himself under the heading of 'history and eschatology' (17-34).

That makes the problem for exegesis more radical. 'For our Gospels believed, in all good faith, that they possessed a tradition about the earthly Lord, which was reliable over wide stretches of its content. Historical criticism has shattered this good faith as far as we ourselves are concerned' (34). 'But even this criticism finds itself in very great methodological difficulties because, apart from the parables, we possess absolutely no kind of formal criteria by which we can identify the authentic Jesus material' (35). 'In only one case do we have more or less safe ground under our feet; when there are no grounds either for deriving a tradition from Judaism or for ascribing it to primitive Christianity, and especially when Jewish Christianity has mitigated or modified the received tradition, as having found it too bold for its taste' (37).

Bultmann had already used such a minimal criterion in his *History of the Synoptic Tradition* (see 3.2.3), albeit expanded by the use of psychological criteria like the 'characteristic mood' of a saying, etc. Käsemann regards this as being 'too bold'. On the basis of this minimal criterion Käsemann then sketches out the 'distinctive element in the mission of Jesus' (37-45), with the conclusion 'that we must look for the distinctive element in the earthly Jesus in his preaching and interpret both his other activities and his destiny in the light of this preaching' (44).

'What is the general sense of this... outline?' (45). 'My own concern is to show that, out of the obscurity of the life story of Jesus, certain characteristic traits in his preaching stand out in relatively sharp relief, and that primitive Christianity united its own message with these. The heart of our problem lies here: the exalted Lord has almost entirely swallowed up the image of the earthly Lord and yet the community maintains the identity of the exalted Lord with the earthly. The solution of this problem cannot, however, if our findings are right, be approached with any hope of success along the line of supposed historical *bruta facta* but only along the line of the connection and tension between the preaching of Jesus and that of his community. The question of the historical Jesus is, in its legitimate form, the question of the continuity of the Gospel within the discontinuity of the ties and within the variation of the kerygma' (46).

If we recall the end of Albert Schweitzer's book (see 2.4.2.4), this no longer means the Jesus who vanishes by Lake Gennesaret and calls men and women to follow him, but the historical Jesus who emerges again from the kerygma, whose preaching, for all its discontinuity and variation, forms the unity not only of theology but also of the kerygma. So the question is no longer what support the kerygma has in the historical Jesus himself; the concern is to examine the kerygma, and then even more the theologies, with reference to the historical Jesus as he is reconstructed by historical-critical exegesis from the Jesus tradition contained in the Gospels.

This article opened up a discussion which in 1960 was summed up and evaluated by Rudolf Bultmann, since it was principally about his conception of theological exegesis (see 3.1.2).

Rudolf Bultmann, 'Das Verhältnis der urchristlichen Christusbotschaft zum historischen Jesus', in *Exegetica*, 1967, 445-69. For those lucky enough to track it down, an English translation is available as 'The Relationship of the Primitive Christian Message of Christ to the Historical Jesus', in *The Historical Jesus and the Kerygmatic Christ*, Nashville 1964, 15-42. Page references here have necessarily to be to the German.

It is first the question of the historical continuity between the activity of the historical Jesus, especially his proclamation, and the primitive

Christian Christ-kerygma. Secondly, it is the question of the relationship in content between Jesus and the kerygma' (446). Bultmann answers the first question with reference to Paul and John, to the effect that the historical continuity does not go beyond the 'fact of his history' (449); the Christ of the kerygma is the historical Jesus, but he is to be reckoned as part of Judaism.

In the question of continuity of content Bultmann first rejects the attempt to show that the 'picture of the person of the historical Jesus and his activity is implicitly contained in the kerygma' (450). The very state of the sources does not allow us to make any portrait of Jesus. What really matters is the opposite question, whether 'the kerygma is already contained *in nuce* in the deeds and words of Jesus' (456). Precisely because it is proclamation, the proclamation of Jesus also has kerygmatic character, but it is not explicit proclamation of Christ. 'One can, however, say that Jesus' emergence and his proclamation imply a christology in so far as he called for a decision about his person as the bearer of the Word of God, a decision on which salvation or damnation depended. The confession of the community given in the kerygma would then have to be understood as the explanation of the response to the question of decision, obedience, which recognizes the revelation of God in Jesus' (457).

However, according to Bultmann such considerations remain in the sphere of historical explanation; it is not the historical Jesus but the kerygma which also reaches other generations directly. For Bultmann it is possible to bridge over history only by means of existentialist intepretation (see 3.1.2.4); only an existentialist interpretation of the proclamation of the historical Jesus, which he feels to have been carried out in exemplary fashion by James M.Robinson (*A New Quest of the Historical Jesus*, SBT 25, SCM Press 1959, reissued with other material by Fortress Press 1983), turns this historical proclamation into an address to the present and thus makes it identical with the kerygma: 'From a formal perspective this identity consists in the fact that Jesus' activity in word and deed confronts men and women with decision in the same way as does the Christ kerygma' (464); the content of this is: 'The message of Jesus, like the kerygma, calls for a break with the old aeon and readiness for the new aeon which is already dawning; bowing before God's judgment and receiving the grace of God' (464).

So why still the kerygma and not a repetition of the proclamation of Jesus? 'The resolution to the problem lies in the fact that the kerygma has changed the "once" of the historical Jesus into the "once for all"; in other words, that the earliest community... understood the history of Jesus as the decisive eschatological event which as such can never become a merely past event but remains present, and does so in proclamation' (467). The church is the vehicle of the kerygma: 'faith in the church as the bearer of the kerygma is the Easter faith which consists in the faith that Jesus Christ is present in the kerygma' (469).

So what is conceded is not just a continuity but an identity in content between the proclamation of the historical Jesus and the kerygma; the kerygma makes Jesus present as the eschatological saving event. However, whereas Bultmann conceded this only on condition that the proclamation of Jesus was interpreted in existentialist terms, in the subsequent period approaches were made which Bultmann here still sought to ward off on the grounds that they were psychological or historical. Even more than Jesus' proclamation, his actions and his underlying intention were taken as a norm for Christianity; interest shifted from Paul and John to the synoptic Gospels. However, here the question remained how far Jesus' actions were binding as a norm and how it was possible to make Jesus present, i.e. how the historical complex in which Jesus lived could be identified by means of historical interpretation in such a way that it was above time and capable of being repeated in the present (to take e.g. the conflicts described in the disputes: how does one identify the opponents of Jesus, the subject of the conflict and Jesus' basic saying as present possibilities?).

Since Bultmann understands theology as 'the conceptual description of human existence as existence governed by God' (see 3.1.2.3), the proclamation of Jesus interpreted in existentialist terms, like the kerygma, would only be among the presuppositions of the theology of the New Testament and not part of that theology. That the theologies of Lohse, Kümmel, Goppelt and, particularly strikingly, Jeremias (since only one volume of it appeared) describe Jesus' proclamation as theology (see.1.3.5) is thus the consequence of another understanding of this concept. Above all, however, what is of course meant by this is that Christian theology has its origins in the proclamation of Jesus.

3.4.3   Hermeneutics

The discussions described in the last two sections come under the heading of 'hermeneutics', as the way of dealing with history and texts associated with theological exegesis in this sense. This heading also covers what elsewhere is described as 'the new concern with history', with which Bultmann, without using the actual term, prefaced his Jesus book in an introduction entitled 'View Point and Method'. If hermeneutics in itself generally denotes a theory of understanding, now the specific reference is to that theory which is defined by Dilthey (see

1.3.2) as 'the artistic theory of the understanding of expressions of life fixed in writing'.

For an introduction to these questions see A.Thiselton, *The Two Horizons*, Paternoster Press and Eerdmans 1980.

In contrast to historicism, the hermeneutical question, put in this way, became the basic question of historical understanding generally, not just in the sphere of theology but in the humanities as a whole (see 1.3.2). It became the basis of the scientific theory underlying them. If the questioning is no longer concerned with historical events as such but with expressions of life, then a pre-understanding on the part of the interpreter is indispensable; the interpreter must know the expression of life which he or she is investigating in order to understand its historical expression (pre-understanding does not mean a pre-judgment or even a false understanding, nor what can be described as interest in an ideological sense). For example, anyone who wants to understand what is meant by love in a historical text by love must know what love is. Under this heading of hermeneutics the task of theology was defined as the understanding of historical texts: hermeneutics was the problem of method generally and was discussed as a problem in scientific theory.

R.Bultmann, 'The Problem of Hermeneutics', in *Essays. Philosophical and Theological*, SCM Press 1955, 234-61;
E.Fuchs, *Hermeneutik*, 1954.

If theology as hermeneutical theology has to do with history and texts, its subject-matter is language. However, since as theology it has to do with the word of God, in this sense hermeneutics is more than an arbitrary, interchangeable historical or linguistic method, but like form criticism it becomes adequate exegetical questioning (see 3.2.3), the 'linguistic theory of faith', as E.Fuchs put it. The hermeneutical problem is not a formal problem, but *the* theological problem.

However, such theological hermeneutics does not differ from hermeneutics generally; the characteristic concern with history, text and language is the same, and there is nothing special in the fact that it too has to do with 'eminent texts'.

For this term see H.G.Gadamer, *Truth and Method*, Sheed and Ward 1981.

Nor does the fact that the biblical texts have a history of influence which has lasted down to the present day set them apart from other 'eminent texts'. The pre-understanding, finally, is not faith as a presupposition for theological understanding but the questionability of human existence.

If exegesis and with it theology generally define themselves in this way as hermeneutics, in Ebeling (see 3.4.1) specifically over against

Catholicism, and in the question of the historical Jesus (see 3.4.2) as part of a concern to make Jesus present, the question arises as to how its specific character is to be distinguished from hermeneutics generally. On the other hand, however, one cannot rule out the possibility that there could be other ways of understanding history, text and language which might compete with hermeneutics in the special sense.

Within exegesis – and not as a chance concomitant of the question of the historical Jesus – hermeneutics had been particularly concerned with the interpretation of the parables of Jesus, because the parables speak of God in terms of basic happenings in life. But their mode of expression is clearly open to other approaches than the hermeneutical approach, however much dispute there may be as to which is the right one.

It proves difficult to incorporate the history of exegesis (Ebeling) or the history of influence (Gadamer) into the interpretation of an individual text; this is clear from the passages where this is meant to happen in commentaries of the Evangelisch-Katholischer Kommentar series, which is based on a programme of such incorporation. By and large there are no preliminary studies in this area. Interpretation and influence can come about in the most varied ways, not just in commentaries or sermons on the text; for the theology of the early church and the Middle Ages, and indeed beyond, dogmatic works are certainly more important here.

The two terms 'interpretation' and 'influence' themselves remain problematical, since they presuppose the pre-eminence of the biblical text and thus an understanding of theology as primarily the exegesis of scrip ure; but that is typically Protestant. Perhaps it would be better to talk of a 'history of mediation', with the main question 'How have bib..cal texts been handed down to us?' This approach would include questions of textual tradition and translation, but above all investigate the theological contexts in which texts are placed (an example in the Protestant sphere is Mark 1.13-16 in connection with baptism, or use of rules for conduct [the so-called 'house-tables'] in the New Testament letters in the context of an ethics of status in sermons about the Christian household).

Peter Stuhlmacher even wants to take the history of influence into exegesis itself with his call for an expansion of Troeltsch's three principles (criticism, analogy and correlation, see 2.4.2.2) by a fourth principle of 'perception'. He takes over this term from Paul Ricoeur, but defines the principle as 'the pendant to methodological doubt which is necessary today. To this doubt (for Troeltsch, criticism) must be added in historical research the readiness to accept and work with the claim of the tradition, its reality-content and the history of its influence.'

P.Stuhlmacher, 'Neues Testament und Hermeneutik', *Zeitschrift für Theologie und Kirche* 68, 1971, 121-61; the quotation is on 148f.

In his book *Vom Verstehen des Neuen Testaments* (On Understanding the New Testament), which explicitly has the term hermeneutics in the subtitle, Stuhlmacher has now focussed this idea on the principle of 'arriving at an understanding with the text'.

P. Stuhlmacher, *Vom Verstehen des Neuen Testaments*, Grundrisse zum Neuen Testament 6, 1979, esp. paragraphs 13 and 14; however, this principle does not just govern his work in §15, but throughout the historical parts of the book.

What is called for is a 'link back to church dogmatics' (210). 'In a church-orientated exegesis of scripture the main data of this history of influence, in the form of the great traditions of the confessions of the church, form a framework which must not be neglected. Within it, now as before, open dialogue can be carried on over the truth with the biblical texts' (221).

But would arriving at an understanding with the text always be to the same degree arriving at an understanding with the church tradition? And can such an understanding be an ethical norm, which would lead exegetes to censor themselves? Can the term hermeneutics be formalized to such a degree that Stuhlmacher can refer back to Barth's and Schlatter's understanding of scripture and at the same time to Troeltsch's principles of historical method? In that case, is the hermeneutical question as such not the theologically adequate question that it is in Ebeling and Fuchs, but just one which relates the pre-understanding from a history of influence interpreted in a particular way)?

3.4.4   The canon and biblical theology

The nineteenth century brought not only the separation of the two exegetical disciplines of Old and New Testaments (1.1.5) but also the reorientation of the presuppositions for understanding the New Testament, which were no longer sought primarily in the Old Testament but in Hellenism and in 'Late' Judaism (see 2.3.3); theologically this then turned into a fundamental questioning of the significance of the Old Testament for theology generally, from Schleiermacher (see the quotation in 1.1.15) to Harnack. Harnack thought that the acceptance of the Old Testament into the canon had been unavoidable in the second century, that its retention by Luther had been understandable, but was now reprehensible – the table had to be 'swept clean'.

Of course this development was also connected with Old Testament exegesis in that in historical-critical terms it led up to Israel and not Christianity. Here too theological exegesis, in which connection special mention should be made of Gerhard von Rad (1901-1971), brought a turning point, and it was called for all the more as a result of antisemitism inside and outside the church.

Whereas the development of individual exegetical questions in both disciplines ran parallel, or New Testament scholars learned from Old Testament scholars – and there were still exegetes who worked in both disciplines, like Wellhausen with his commentaries on the synoptic Gospels (see 2.2.4) – here the ways parted: to put things simply, the theological exegesis of the Old Testament was more closely related to the theology of Karl Barth than to that of Bultmann; thematically the concepts of revelation and salvation history came to the fore.

Whereas in the third part of his two-volume *Old Testament Theology* (Oliver and Boyd and Harper and Row 1962, 1965, reissued SCM Press 1975) von Rad builds a bridge to the New Testament and sees the Old Testament 'as a book in which expectation keeps mounting up to vast proportions' (319), and the New Testament as 'ringing with the exultant awareness of standing in a new era of God's activity' (329), which was at the same time the actualization of the old expectations, there is nothing similar in the theological exegesis of the New Testament shaped by hermeneutics.

In his 1933 article on 'The Significance of the Old Testament for Christian Faith', after describing the Old Testament Bultmann begins with the hermeneutical question, 'what basic possibility it presents for an understanding of human existence' (13) – 'this understanding of existence is the same as that of the New Testament' (20). 'To the Christian faith the Old Testament is no longer revelation as it has been, and still is, for the Jews' (31). 'To the Christian faith the Old Testament is not in the true sense God's Word. So far as the church proclaims the Old Testament as God's word, it just finds in it again what is already known from the revelation in Jesus Christ' (32). But this leaves open the question whether it might not be better to begin directly from the New Testament.

R.Bultmann, 'The Significance of the Old Testament for the Christian Faith', in B.W.Anderson, *The Old Testament and Christian Faith*, Harper and Row and SCM Press 1964, 8-35; in my view the 1949 article 'Prophecy and Fulfilment' (in *Essays on Old Testament Interpretation*, John Knox Press and SCM Press 1963, 89-122) does not match the earlier article.

The 1969 article by Philipp Vielhauer, 'Paulus und das Alte Testament', is representative of the strictly exegetical sphere because it was so influential; according to Vielhauer the Old Testament is not a significant element in Pauline theology, but Paul uses the Old Testament only against its real sense and for his own purposes.

P.Vielhauer, 'Paulus und das Alte Testament', in id., *Oikodome*, ed. G.Klein, Theologische Bücherei 65, 1979, 196-228.

Vielhauer generalizes fom this 'that the fact of the two-part canon is not a hermeneutical principle in accordance with which one has to intepret the Old Testament in the light of the New and the New Testament in the light of the Old' – only the latter would have any significance for New Testament exegesis. He stresses this statement, after a dash, with the warning: 'this would notoriously lead to doing violence to the texts on both sides, e.g. in respect of the law and the messiah' (228) – evidently a free gift on both sides, but one which is made wholly at the expense of the Old Testament. So the discussion is carried on only about the canon of the New Testament, under the headings 'centre of scripture' or 'canon in the canon'.

Cf. the collected volume *Das Neue Testament als Kanon*, ed. E.Käsemann, Göttingen 1970;
cf. also Brevard S.Childs, *The New Testament as Canon: An Introduction*, SCM Press and Fortress Press 1984.

Similarly, however, in the sphere of Old Testament exegesis the discussion about the 'centre of the Old Testament' has largely been carried on without including the New. In the case of the New Testament this discussion is dominated by the headings 'hermeneutics', kerygma and historical Jesus, the negative counterpart to which is 'early Catholicism' as a departure from what was original (however that might be defined) that can already be noted in the New Testament.

All in all, the problem of the canon evidently does not play a major role either historically or theologically; on the historical side that is clear from the Introductions (see 1.3.5), in which (Kümmel excepted) there is hardly any real account of the origin of the canon – nor is it among the basic knowledge which textbooks seek to communicate.

Nevertheless, at present two tendencies can be noted. On the one hand is the transcending of the concept of canon as a matter of principle, which is most clearly documented for English-speaking readers in Helmut Koester's *Introduction to the New Testament* (see 1.3.5). Unlike other introductions, this describes all early Christian literature up to about 130/150 CE. Koester's basic requirement is that 'the distinctions between canonical and non-canonical, orthodox and heretical literature are things of the past. The classical "Introduction to the New Testament" has lost its scientific justification. One can really speak only of a "History of Early Christian Literature".'

See H.Koester and J.M.Robinson, *Trajectories through Early Christianity*, Fortress Press 1971, 270.

Instead of the reduction intended in the discussion about the 'canon in the canon', here we in fact have an extension: early Christianity does not comprise just a single kerygma but also the heretics who are fought against in the New Testament and the writings which were not included in the canon. Would early Christianity have to be defined in different terms if the canon looked different?

Here the basic argument advanced by Walter Bauer has come into particular prominence. He claimed that there was no orthodoxy at the beginning of Christianity, but that orthodoxy was, rather, a norm which was only defined at the end of early Christianity. His book appeared in 1934 – the wrong time, since 1934 was the year in which the Protestant church for the first time again marked itself off from heresy, in the Theological Declaration of Barmen.

W.Bauer, *Orthodoxy and Heresy in Earliest Christianity* (1934), English translation Fortress Press and SCM Press 1971.

Käsemann took up Bauer's thesis with the provocative question 'Is the New Testament Canon the Basis of the Unity of the Church?' and replied 'No, but rather of the multiplicity of the Christian churches'.

E.Käsemann, 'The Canon of the New Testament and the Unity of the Church', in *Essays on New Testament Themes*, SCM Press 1964, 95-107.

On the other hand, Stuhlmacher combines the programme of a 'biblical theology' with his 'hermeneutics of arriving at an understanding' in the sense of a connection between the New Testament and the Old which is not only historical but also one of content. Here the term 'biblical theology' does not so much mean a contrast to dogmatic theology as a theology common to both Testaments, developed under the heading of 'reconciliation' (this is the model in the closing paragraph of his *Hermeneutics*).

Starting from Gerhard von Rad's traditio-historical interpretation, and in close collaboration with the Old Testament scholar Hartmut Gese, Stuhlmacher outlines a connection between Old Testament and New in terms of the history of tradition. Gese describes this as an ontological extension, i.e. no longer a handing down of content nor just a context for understanding the world and humankind. The Old Testament ends up in the New; but the New Testament is only to be understood in the context of this development.

Particularly if one does not reject the theme of 'biblical theology' in principle, as largely happens in New Testament exegesis, a series of questions remains:

- Does the connection between Old and New Testaments not lie more in particular shared questions about God, humankind and the world than in an identity of theological statements?
- How are we to evaluate the transition from early Christianity into the Greek world which presupposes a similar transition from Judaism into the Greek world?
- Does the Old Testament really end up only in the New Testament, and not also in rabbinic Judaism which began to take shape after 70, or in Jewish apocalyptic?

3.4.5   Ethics

The main difference between theological exegesis and historical theology lay in the completely different status of ethics: both Barth and Bultmann noted it at this point (3.1). In Bultmann this is particularly evident in the article described at 3.1.2.2. On the other hand this is also the main criticism of theological exegesis these days: it is accused of having no significance for ethics. That is not, of course, meant as a moral indictment against Bultmann as an individual, but as an objection to the content of theology as governed by hermeneutics, which does not see ethics as a distinctive theological theme.

This problem is again closely connected with the end of historical theology which was described in 2.4, and not least with the question of the significance of the historical Jesus. That Jesus' proclamation is essentially ethics is one of the differences between Jesus and the kerygma. Albert Schweitzer (see 2.4.2.4) described this ethics as interim ethics, i.e. as ethics only for the intermediate period until the coming of the End, after which ethics would no longer be necessary. In that case, however, the content of ethics can no longer have direct significance once the presupposition, namely the imminence of the end, no longer exists; hence Friedrich Naumann's theological objection (see 2.4.3).

The form-critical thesis put forward above all by Dibelius belongs in the exegetical sphere (see 3.2.3). Dibelius argued that ethics is a secondary theme in early Christian writings; only after the fading of the imminent expectation were the form and content of ethics taken over from contemporary Hellenistic material by way of Hellenistic Judaism – this is the history-of-religions theory. So ethics proved to be a secondary theme from an exegetical perspective as well.

Bultmann took up this theme systematically in his 1924 article 'The Problem of Ethics in Paul'.

'Das Problem der Ethik bei Paulus', *ZNW* 23, 123-40, reprinted in R.Bultmann, *Exegetica*, 1967, 36-54, to which the page numbers refer.

The article begins with an objection to historical theology, which in Bultmann's view can only note a contradiction between justification and ethics. But the starting point must be that 'Paul bases the imperative on the fact of justification and derives the imperative from the indicative' (39). Whereas historical theology – and Bultmann uses the ethics of the Stoa as a history-of-religions analogy – saw the identity of the human being achieved only through his action, by contrast Bultmann describes the consequence of the Pauline doctrine of justification as being: 'the identity of the one who is justified with the empirical person is a matter of *faith*. As the concrete, empirical person (the one who, seen from the perspective of God, is a sinner) is justified and has sin forgiven, the relationship between the one who is justified and the beyond does not exist apart from or alongside the specific action and fate of this individual' (50). The action of the one who is justified is then obedience; the content of the demand of obedience is not new; men and women know what they have to do and need no specifically Christian ethics. But they are to do what they know has to be done.

Such a conception frees men and women from always having to achieve their own identity only by means of their actions, and it certainly had ethical consequences, since Bultmann was very well aware of what had to be said and done in 1933.

The relatively few works in Protestantism on New Testament ethics modify this exegetical and systematic approach, but do not in principle put it in question. Cf. especially W.Schrage, *The Ethics of the New Testament*, Fortress Press and T.& T.Clark 1988; for the English-speaking world see J.L.Houlden, *Ethics in the New Testament*, Mowbray 1973.

– But now the question what is to be done has become particularly difficult: is the history-of-religions model of 'taking over the ethics of that time' to be understood as also involving an adoption for the present of the ethical aims then on offer, to which Christians would be even more obligated?
– Another difficult question is whether the apocalyptic horizon of the proclamation of Jesus is just historically conditioned. Has Christian ethics, for example, to formulate an interim ethic in view of the threat of the end of the world?
– In this way, what theology really is has also become questionable, and this question leads to the 'further questions'.

4   Further Questions

4.1   The relationships of exegesis

The history of exegesis has more facets than are depicted in this book. The reason why Part 3 is so strongly orientated on Bultmann as an exegete is that his work is the most evocative example of the controversy with historical theology and in him the themes of exegetical and theological discussion seem to come together. I have not used the term 'aporia' in connection with theological exegesis in 3.4 as I did in connection with historical theology in 2.4, first because these issues are so recent, but above all because the aporias of historical theology can only be seen as aporias in the light of theological exegesis.

However, it still seems to me that in principle theological exegesis cannot be replaced by 'alternative' forms of exegesis and their concern with understanding rather than explanation. The open questions in 3.4 culminate in the question of the significance of the historical Jesus; they involve not only as it were 'purely' exegetical questions – in principle these can be resolved – but not least the question of the nature of theology and the church. Therefore what we have here is neither an exegetical or a theological aporia, but an open question. It seems to me open whether the hermeneutical question or the ethical question should be seen as aporias; others might well say that they were.

If this book has been an attempt to take up and reflect on the history of exegesis, its aim cannot be viewed as an attempt to overcome the crisis of New Testament exegesis sketched out in 1.3.3 by turning away from this history, as the 'end of historical-critical exegesis', in whatever way that may be evoked. But we do need to think once again about the changed field of exegesis which is addressed there.

Exegesis is done in relation not only to theology as a whole but also to other disciplines, to church and school. If this field changes and with it the questions put to exegesis, the result is not simply an adaptation to the changes but a controversy with them which does not simply take them as given but rather takes part in the change – and does not just put a brake on it. What was described in 1.3.3 is not a closed process but in itself a matter of dispute. There is a recognizable tendency to lay more store by the term 'experience' – how this is to be done is much disputed, as is what is meant by 'experience'. New Testament exegesis must take part in this dispute.

The most elementary point of dispute which also emerges behind the theme of experience is whether scholarship is to be pursued as understanding or as the formation of theories orientated on action, and this dispute has come to involve the whole field of New Testament exegesis. However, at this point such scholarship does not need to resign and see itself as a now outmoded fashion; in its own heritage it has enough arguments and indeed questions to cope with the dispute over the alternatives of understanding and (mere) explanation.

Exegesis with its concern with historical texts is also affected by the 'new' disciplines of linguistics, sociology and psychology. None of them is a closed discipline; on the contrary, there are disputes between different schools in all of them. That does not rule them out, but it does rob them of a little of the unanimity and power that they claim and prevents exegesis from being intimidated by any of them. The same is true of similar changes of field in the history of exegesis; it has not just been altered by these changes but has also introduced the changes itself.

The questions in 2.4 and 3.4 are not only said to be 'open' but are also meant to be 'open'. They may occasionally be suggestive, in which case perhaps my own position comes through more clearly than I had intended; however, they are not meant to suggest a verdct but to challenge the reader to a verdict.

4.2 Linguistics

New Testament exegesis has to do with texts and languages. So it is always related to the linguistic disciplines, and especially of course to classical philology. The special lexicons and grammars (see 1.2.4) refer to similar lexicons and grammars of the Greek language; since the Reformation there has been close collaboration here, which of course also went with the importance attached to Greek in schools and in other disciplines (whereas nowadays Greek usually has to be learned 'afterwards' by theological students and is hardly needed in other disciplines). But literary criticism also includes linguistic elements; it has a particular linguistic usage as one of its criteria; so does form criticism, which takes the Jesus tradition as an expression of collective narration and does not investigate the particular language of individual authors. Linguistic considerations above all underlie the programme of the *Theological Dictionary of the New Testament* (see 2.3.3); in its stress on etymology for the significance of words it is indebted to a particular trend in the comparative study of languages which seeks the 'real' meaning of a word in its etymology.

But the identification of word and concept was also grounded in the study of language. At this point the more recent study of languages, termed linguistics, has so far had the most lasting impact on New Testament exegesis; the term concept (German *Begriff*) has almost completely disappeared from it (though the replacement of 'concept' by 'term' [the same word in both English and German] is not in itself a matter of linguistics). The most significant book here has been James Barr's *The Semantics of Biblical Language*, Oxford University Press 1961, reissued SCM Press 1983.

In particular Barr criticized the programme of *TDNT* for taking the Greek words of the New Testament as concepts, as if they always stood for wider firm theological contexts. Since then there have been no further 'investigations of concepts'; they have been replaced by investigations of complexes of motives or traditions, above all in history-of-religions questions. These are no longer primarily orientated on the Greek words.

That has had consequences beyond the purely methodological question, since on the one hand Bultmann had defined theology as the 'conceptual description of human existence as governed by God', and his *Theology of the New Testament* was built up specifically on Greek words understood as such concepts. But in that case where does one get the concepts from, or is theology to be developed on quite a different basis? Is 'narrative theology' the only alternative?

Textual linguistics has had a less lasting effect, perhaps because both classical form criticism with its interpretation of the Gospel and at least the beginnings of an attempt to see a relationship between the letters and rhetorical traditions in the so-called 'diatribe style' had already made a start in this direction. On the other hand, it is necessary in principle to maintain the thesis which underlies literary criticism, that the Gospels stand at the end of a process of tradition which has many levels. But perhaps the basic disagreement in the redaction-critical interpretation of the Gospel of Mark can be overcome (see 3.3.3) if work does not go on here with the scheme of tradition and redaction which has been tried with Matthew and Luke but there is a search for inner references and relationships within the Gospel of Mark which are present in the passion predictions – and not only there.

4.3 ·   Psychology

Exegesis has to do with texts which not only speak of contexts of life but also have underlying contexts in life. Now from the beginning theological exegesis has gone hand in hand with polemic against psychology. That was part of the front it presented to historical theology, which legitimated itself in a Jesus reconstructed in historical and psychological terms, but also sought to make theological contexts like justification psychologically comprehensible. Not only exegesis, but also dogmatics and practical theology are sharply distinguished from psychology in dialectical theology; this is opposition not just to the nineteenth-century trend but also to psychoanalysis of a Freudian type (that of Jung is far more acceptable).

This theology was characterized by negatives (for Bultmann see 3.1.2.4) which were meant to prevent a psychological understanding, e.g. of faith. There were very different motives for this, but they unite in opposition to any psychological (or even 'psychologizing') explanation and calculation of contexts in life. Any attempt at a psychological interpretation of these contexts would be a criticism of religion which even affected a theology which dissociated itself from religion.

Now of course it is impossible simply to brand as heresy the possibility of a psychological interpretation. The methodological problem arises in connection with New Testament texts as to how far a discipline built on the interaction between client and psychologist can be concerned with texts and indeed historical texts. But the methodological problem is not insoluble in principle if no more is required than the degree of plausibility which is also recognized as being sufficient elsewhere in the historical sciences. For example, when in Romans 7 Paul talks so emphatically about the history of an ego, the reader has psychological associations which need to be clarified, even if psychological approaches are not a great deal of help in interpretation – precisely because they differ so much.

It is simpler to integrate psychological questioning into a particular sphere of history-of-religions work. If in theological exegesis conceptions are not derived from anywhere, but relate connections in the history of religion to universal questions, then these questions also have a psychological content. Certainly existentialia like care, anxiety, and so on do not denote primarily psychological phenomena, but existentialist philosophy nevertheless has a relationship to psychology. The high emotional value, say, of the 'undogmatic' christology of the 'I am' sayings in the Gospel of John – the good shepherd, the way, the truth, etc. – is already important for exegesis.

However, psychological factors already come into play in the reading or the hearing. This is more than a matter of triggering off associations; it is also a matter of how such a text is experienced – as confirmation, as threat, etc. (see 1.3.1). Exegesis has the aim of leading beyond such associations and feelings so that the understanding is not blocked by them; but it only achieves this aim if it reflects these factors (which are rather different from pre-understanding in the classical hermeneutical sense, see 3.4.3).

Finally, it is important for exegesis itself to be rooted in developmental psychology. Its context is still predominantly at the beginning of study, i.e. at the phase when students are breaking free of the ties of home, friendship and community which previously bound them; the critical potential of exegesis coincides with this and evidently has always made exegesis attractive as such. The change of the scope of exegesis has meant that it plays a significantly smaller role in any new integration into family, friendship and community during the second phase of theological education.

4.4   Sociology

Finally, New Testament exegesis is concerned with those contexts in which social relationships come about. That is true both of the texts and of the practice of exegesis itself. Theological exegesis has stressed this over against historical theology with its form-critical question about the community as the vehicle of the tradition (see 3.2.3) and at the same time has understood itself as a discipline related to the church. Although as a result its distance from sociology has been essentially less than that from psychology, sociological questions hardly ever arise.

In principle a sociological explanation of the phenomenon of early Christianity would also be a criticism of religion which affected even this theology, whether it derived the origin of Christianity from particular conditions which can be described by sociology or explained exegetes themselves in sociological terms. The Marxist criticism of religion in particular is moving in this direction.

Now early Christianity as a historical phenomenon is not above sociological interpretation. Even if the origin of Christianity does not lie in a group which understands itself in social or political terms, and if such a self-understanding is not formulated expressly for the sphere of early Christianity, from the beginning Christianity has had social and political implications. At any rate the Roman state interpreted it as such a phenomenon, as is shown by the earliest Roman texts that we have (Suetonius, Tacitus, Pliny and Trajan). The mere fact that proclamation leads to the formation of communities and not just to an individual new orientation is a social phenomenon which can be investigated – again with the proviso that judgments are merely plausible.

G.Theissen in particular has done this in his *Studien zur Soziologie des Urchristentum* (Studies on the Sociology of Earliest Christianity), SUNT 19, 1979 (see 3-34 for an introduction to 'the place of sociological questioning in the history of research'). The point of contact can be the history-of-religions questioning which was formalized in 2.3.4, if it investigates not only connections with cultural history but also the social history of the time, and here it generally meets up with a corresponding interest in historical research.

The relationship of exegesis to a sociology which understands itself as a theory orientated on action is more difficult. Here the fundamental difference in scholarly orientation remains – is it to be understanding or theorizing? But here too the problem of the basis of ethics also plays a part – it is still unclear whether there is a specific Christian ethic which develops its own norms (and are these to be binding only on Christians or on everyone?), or whether Christian ethics develops norms from elsewhere and gives them authoritative support (in which case, which norms has it taken over and which not?). On the other hand, in the meantime the dispute as to whether ethics is social or individualistic rightly seems to have become a thing of the past, though the dispute over political ethics is coming to a head because questions of principle have not been sorted out.

4.5   Exegesis in new relationships

The sketch of the context of New Testament exegesis in a changed environment which has been given here is subjectively a sketch by one exegete reflecting on further questions. I have mentioned only two books in this last section, both of which are already widely accepted; I have not engaged in polemic, nor have I referred to works of my own in which exegesis takes up these further questions on my own behalf in connection with theological exegesis. This book does not set out to confront a particular position, but to make the reader reflect on the New Testament itself.

DATE DUE